A New Marriage, A New Life

ALSO BY FREDERIC F. FLACH, M.D.

THE SECRET STRENGTH OF DEPRESSION

CHOICES: COPING CREATIVELY WITH PERSONAL CHANGE

A New Marriage, A New Life

Frederic F. Flach, M.D.

McGRAW-HILL BOOK COMPANY
NEW YORK • ST. LOUIS • SAN FRANCISCO
DÜSSELDORF • MEXICO • TORONTO

Book design by Barbara Hall.

2 3 4 5 6 7 8 9 0 FGRFGR 7 8 3 2 1 0 9 8

Library of Congress Cataloging in Publication Data

Flach, Frederic F
A new marriage, a new life.
Includes index.
1. Remarriage—United States. I. Title
HQ1018.S4F53 301.42'7 77-27976
ISBN 0-07-021250-3

TO JOYCE

This book is really hers. For, however valuable, objective insights discovered in a professional context can be truly understood only by the experience of living them.

Contents

Introduction

It was not so long ago that many of us knew few divorced and remarried people. Our friends, business and social acquaintances, we ourselves seemed pretty well settled into first and only marriages, for better or worse. Now what was once an isolated phenomenon has become commonplace, and millions of divorced men and women are seriously considering new marriages—if they have not begun them already.

As a psychiatrist, I have seen the number of people seeking advice in helping to adjust to divorce rise sharply over the last ten years. Many couples who now come for marital counseling are already married again, fearful that these relationships too may fall apart. In one way or another, they are all afraid, demoralized and depressed. And why not? After all, depression is a normal human response to real or anticipated loss, whether of something or someone valued or the loss of our own self-esteem. We are confronted with the challenge of overcoming depression and regaining self-confidence, while, at the same time, actively redesigning our lives.

I am convinced that if people in second marriages were more familiar with the stresses they have to cope with, more schooled in handling depression, and more creative in establishing their new lives, the quality and durability of their marriages could be significantly enhanced. Studies have conclusively shown that the more prepared we are to cope with change, the more effectively we can do so.

Hope springs eternal, although without common sense it can readily become myopic optimism. Unfortunately, and at considerable risk to our futures, most of us tend to muddle along. For regardless of how sensible the decision to end a bad marriage may be, the fact is that our new lives will be difficult. And second marriages, however well selected and however much they represent a real chance for happiness, bring with them an even more complex group of problems than many first ones do. Moreover, within the framework of any marriage a couple's relationship is never static; it evolves in stages. Only by learning to be insightful and flexible can we weather these turning points successfully.

No matter where you are in the cycle of marriage, divorce, remarriage, you can transform the odds against success into a high likelihood of making your new life work by exploring and answering a few basic questions. Even if you cannot come up with answers right away, at least you will have taken a first step toward doing so.

To begin with, should you marry again at all? Or would it be better for you to stay single?

Is your choice of someone to marry really a free and sensible choice? Or is it being influenced by unresolved conflicts and residual attachments to your former marriage or spouse? Or are there other motives deeply buried within you that, if not recognized, will lead you to another misfortune?

Are you ready to deal with the problems that will

confront you the second time? Do you know what these are? Have you cultivated enough insight—into yourself, into your partner, into your life situation? Are you practicing a genuinely creative approach to your life so that you can commit yourself to this new marriage not just once, but again and again?

Are your ideas about the expectations and responsibilities of marriage sufficiently defined so that you can withstand the negative image of marriage and family life that nowadays so often and so unfairly places marriage in such a bad light?

There are no easy solutions, much as we wish there could be. But there are some guidelines and a body of knowledge and experience to help us adjust to divorce and remarriage more intelligently.

I have structured this book around the theme of loss and renewal. Everyone who experiences the ending of one marriage and is struggling to build a new life, whether single or remarried, inevitably goes through some degree of depression. There are certain signs of this emotional state you can look for to determine whether it is still influencing your behavior, and if it is, there are concrete steps you can take to deal with it. By the same token, as you enter new life situations, it is critical for you to learn how to use established methods to stimulate creativity in your thinking and action, so that the life you establish will be meaningful and well suited to your personal needs.

Marrying again takes courage. When you make this decision, you will want to be as prepared as you can. I have identified many of the pitfalls that people reconsidering marriage will encounter—being unduly influenced by resentment or loneliness, for example, or being governed by largely unconscious themes that may have caused failure in previous marriages. I have also described how you can reduce the impact of such influences, thereby increasing your chances of making a better choice.

Once you marry again, you often face a much more complicated set of human relationships than you did before. This can be very stressful. Your new marriage will be affected by people from your past, in fact and in memory, former husbands and former wives and children who are forever yours. For parents, the task of integrating children from previous marriages into new ones can be quite problematic. You will have to plan carefully to work out an honest and effective family policy to carry this off well. Here again, I have described what you can expect and offered some guidelines you can follow to increase the chances that your children will not be adversely affected by remarriage but, rather, as is often the case, may benefit from the new family structure you create. And once the initial adjustment period is over, your new marriage will be subject to the normal ebb and flow of all intimate relationships—again the cycle of loss and renewal, the need to tolerate disruptions and rebuild closeness as the years go by—and the sounder your philosophy regarding marriage is and the more skilled you can become in the art of reconciliation, the stronger your marriage will be.

In today's world, we must all learn to live with uncertainty. At the same time, we have to take on life with the energy and dedication required to make it worthwhile. That's what this book is really about. Successful second marriages are among the best examples of successful coping in action.

Acknowledgments

In the preparation of the material in this book, I wish to thank Gladys Carr of McGraw-Hill for her insightful and remarkably intuitive direction, Heather Barbash for her devoted effort on behalf of realism and structure, and Wilhemina Marvel for her fine editorial tuning. It would be imprudent, it seems to me, for any man to undertake a book on marriage without the continuous infusion of the woman's perspective throughout the process.

A New Marriage, A New Life

1

The Changing Face of Marriage

How did Americans feel about marriage a generation ago? If we take a look at that sensitive barometer of social change, film, we can see that Hollywood's message was that everyone—except for the movie stars themselves and the very rich—was expected to marry and stay married. Even when the subject was divorce, it was usually presented as a highly controversial and undesirable alternative. In the comedy *The Philadelphia Story*, divorce was an element in the script, but the unspoken message was that it was really a game and that Katharine Hepburn, a headstrong young woman who divorced her equally capricious husband (Cary Grant), knew perfectly well she belonged with him, as did the audience.

As recently as ten years ago, a forty-two-year-old accountant described his humiliation on going through a divorce in these words: "I felt terribly self-conscious for months, like going around with some physical deformity. I felt like a social outcast. Filling out any form, like a passport application, meant having to deal with the box marked 'marital status,' and at that point I'd freeze. I didn't take my wedding ring off for six months. The fact that most of our friends avoided me didn't help. My best friend himself made it clear that he'd be glad to have lunch with me now and then, but his wife was so upset by the divorce that I shouldn't expect to be asked to their home."

Times have certainly changed. Being divorced and unmarried attracts little, if any, attention now from most people and, not uncommonly, enthusiastic support from a few. The conviction that marriage is a permanent and sacred thing seems to have vanished. It is Ingmar Bergman in *Scenes from a Marriage* who tells us what married life is really like—a grotesque and horrifying unraveling of a human relationship. Leaving the theater, we are haunted by Liv Ullmann's performance. We try to console ourselves by enumerating people whose marriages we think are pretty good, only to find them hard to count beyond the fingers of one hand.

Although most people are still married, they have been growing steadily more convinced that marriage is not to be trusted. In fact, there is a curious and widespread assumption that few people can find happiness in marriage because the bond itself ruins any excitement and whatever love may have been there at the start. "It's built into the commitment," commented a thirty-two-year-old woman, a dress designer whose first marriage had fallen apart. "I live with a man now. We get along fabulously, but I'd never marry him. If I did, we'd probably start taking each other for granted. I wouldn't feel free. We'd come to resent each other, and it would be over in no time." Once seen as the natural outcome of romance and the legitimate ambition of every college senior, marriage is more likely to be viewed now as a tricky and often dangerous obstacle course leading to disenchantment, boredom, or the open warfare of George and Martha in *Who's Afraid of Virginia Woolf?*

How has the institution of marriage fallen into such disrepute in the United States during the last twenty years? To begin with, marriage is by no means the only social institution we have found wanting. The ethics and behavior of our politicians, businessmen, and academicians have been anything but inspiring. But marriage has been the special victim of the recent trend toward individual freedom and self-fulfillment whatever the cost. In this highly mobile culture, any commitment that seems to interfere with personal goals is viewed as a hindrance to such self-fulfillment. Moreover, the emphasis is not just on freedom but on freedom now. Although seldom put into words as such nowadays, the conviction that time is running out lies behind the urgency for immediate solutions.

The influence of traditional social and religious codes that once provided strong support for the permanence of marriage has diminished. The promise of happiness in some other life, if we do not find it here, is no longer enough to sustain us.

At the same time, our culture has become more tolerant of different life-styles. It is now all right to be single, divorced or never married, illegitimate by birth, homosexual, religious, agnostic. It is even all right to be married. Not only does this flexibility offer us alternatives that we can embrace without embarrassment, but it also highlights the heterogeneous character of society. Numerous studies of group dynamics indicate that when homogeneity or sameness decreases, the cohesiveness or strength of the bonds among the people in the group is less. The forces that once inherently held many marriages and families together are weakened as society becomes so diversified

Small wonder, then, that many people are unwilling to accept their marital difficulties with old-fashioned equanimity. "My husband was hopelessly unreliable with money," said a twenty-nine-year-old woman. "We have two children. He was violently opposed to my working. I felt constantly insecure. We were always being harassed by bill collectors. Some of those credit-card operations make a point of calling the home and getting the wife on the phone to stir her up and push her husband to pay. It nearly drove me crazy. I'm sure my mother would have just put up with it. Instead, I found it easier for me to get a divorce. I have a job. I didn't take any alimony. My husband sends child-support checks each month, and I know exactly how much I can count on."

Perhaps the most significant pressure placed on contemporary marriage is a fundamental shift in the standards against which the success of marriage is measured. What were once central considerations—economic stability, similarity in social backgrounds, the building of a way of life together, shared friends, children—have given way to a new scale, one that focuses hard and almost exclusively on the quality of the interpersonal relationship between the husband and wife. This shift in emphasis has originated in no small measure with women. Until recently, most women were largely confined to the home. Their husbands, on the other hand, lived in two worlds, one domestic, the other work. They were, therefore, freer to ignore problems within their families. But for nonworking women, such escape was impossible. Moreover, it was only logical, though not always accurate, for women to blame whatever unhappiness they might feel on the only environment they knew—their marriages.

Furthermore, if Swiss psychiatrist Carl Jung was correct in his impression, women have traditionally been more in touch with feelings than men. They have valued interpersonal relationships more. Men, Jung observed, were generally more practical and analytical in their approach to problems. It is no surprise, then, that women have been most active in scrutinizing the human aspects of family life and insistent on coming to terms with the psychological issues involved.

The growth of the behavioral sciences has fueled their determination. Even when this influence is neither conscious nor acknowledged, its effect is enormous. Like it or not, we all live with Spock in the nursery, Eric Berne in the living room and at the office, and with Freud and Masters and Johnson in the bedroom. Theories of personality and methods to improve interpersonal relationships—from the concept of the unconscious ("what you're saying now is not what you really mean") to transactional analysis ("I'm O.K., you're not")—have intruded on our lives, sometimes to clarify, sometimes to confuse, but always make us ask: "Is my marriage good enough?"

There is a good reason to ask this question. The kind of marital relationship one has profoundly affects one's physical and mental health. A poor relationship between a husband and wife not only sets the stage for neurotic problems or worse but also for a host of psychosomatic illnesses such as migraine headaches, high blood pressure, and gastric ulcers. A conflict-riddled marriage can also produce enough stress to aggravate coronary heart disease and even lead to sudden and unexpected death.

Self-image is clearly affected. We all see ourselves through the eyes of those close to us. If we are regarded with love and respect and perceived as attractive and periodically told so, we are likely to feel O.K. If, on the other hand, we are exposed to repeated criticisms, hurtful remarks, neglect or the absence of any support or praise, we are likely to doubt ourselves seriously or, in self-defense, retaliate in kind.

The nature of the marital relationship colors the rearing of children. Certain family structures are more likely to produce healthy children. Others are prone to generate problem children who later become problem adults. In our culture, too great a power imbalance, for example, in which either the father or the mother looms larger than and effectively diminishes the other partner, is one such detrimental family organization. Parents who do not or cannot directly express feelings and ideas afford no model for children to learn from, leaving them with limited effectiveness in understanding or managing their own emotions. Sexual difficulties between parents set children up subliminally for having sexual problems themselves as adults.

The concern of some people, however, is seldom so altruistic. Primarily preoccupied with themselves, they view their marriages almost exclusively with regard to whether they help or hinder their own chances for personal happiness. In the discotheques, in the early 1960s, men and women began to dance without touching each other. Millions sit in front of the televison, night after night, mesmerized, in what has been called by some a masturbatory equivalent. Human contact has been reduced and self-absorption nourished.

There is a delicate balance between developing yourself and caring for others. Some people have been able to change their outlooks and embark on new lives without having to break the commitments they have made to their marriages. They do not experience personal growth and attachment to another as mutually exclusive. In some instances, however, the marital relationship has indeed been a barrier to personal development. But too often it is perceived so without sufficient reason. As long as a couple remains obsessed with the confinement marriage represents, they seem unable to consider appropriate options. The partner becomes the enemy, to struggle against and ultimately defeat. Caring is replaced with a self-determination that verges on or, in fact, becomes outright selfishness, and they adopt a policy that proclaims: "I am going to do what I want to do when I want to do it." So, if we look at film again, this time the highly popular *Cousin Cousine*, we see the main characters driven, in a sense, to find happiness together. Despite any motives justifying their affair, there is a highly questionable final scene in which they leave their assembled families, children included, and retire to an upstairs bedroom in a very obvious manner. The striking thing, irrespective of the quality of the film, is that the characters are going beyond lines of ordinary decency and discretion and that the audience seems unaffected by the fact that this is happening.

As we are freed of the need to play roles once imposed on us by society, tradition, and our own families, many of us have been caught up in a frenzied search for self-fulfillment. Some find the ambiguity of this transition intolerable and retreat to new roles. They may, for example, begin to look at the marriage bond as a labor-management contract, imposing written rules and agreements more suited to the automobile workers' union and General Motors than to an intimate and complex human relationship. Others are left floundering, unsure. "Before, I felt oppressed by my sense of responsibility for everything that happened in our home," commented a forty-two-year-old woman. "I was just a few years too late to be influenced by the women's movement in college. I'm too young to look on things the way my mother did. Things were simpler for her. She had no choice. I have one, and I don't know what to do with it."

In spite of the problems that plague contemporary marriage, however, people do not seem to be abandoning marriages rashly. A significant proportion of divorces occur between young men and women, still in their twenties and without children, who feel after a year or two of living together that they have made a mistake and wish to rectify it. Among older people there are usually rather serious and forceful reasons for a marriage's dissolution—years of incompatibility and poor communication, alcoholism, outright and repeated cruelty. Well-defined psychiatric disorders, such as the so-called schizophrenias and manic-depressive reactions, also take their toll.

An experienced divorce attorney has said: "Until the last fifteen years there were only two major reasons why people divorced. Either they had to get out of a really unbearable situation, a vicious, sadistic husband or an alcoholic wife, for example, or for the explicit purpose of marrying someone else with whom they had been having an affair. These are still the most common reasons.

"However, I do see more and more people divorcing because of personal dissatisfaction. They don't get along, or have little in common once the children are grown, or sex is dead. I see women especially who feel they have kept things going on account of the children and don't want to put up with it any longer, even when their husbands desperately want to keep the marriage together. By and large, especially when there are children in the picture, people don't end marriages lightly. What is remarkable is the continuing strength of the bond that holds couples together."

In spite of the rising divorce rate, the emphasis on the

interpersonal quality of marriage and the movement for instant and total self-fulfillment, there seem to be more people who disagree than agree with Margaret Mead's suggestion that marriage may have become an anthropologic curiosity. Most men and women still prefer to be married. As the number of disintegrating marriages burgeons, the number of remarriages moves upward as well.

The majority of swinging bachelors around town, whom we imagine to be recovering from their divorces by dividing their time between glamorous dinner parties and the theater, always in the company of a new and beautiful young woman, are, in fact, usually at home fixing dinner for themselves or watching a rerun on televison of a Humphrey Bogart movie or devoting every weekend to their children. Although they are very much on guard and not without scars from their former marriages, their common goal is to find someone with whom to share their lives. And the average divorced woman, no matter how well adjusted she may be in her career, usually wonders, at the end of a busy day, how many years are left before her youngest child leaves home and she will be totally alone.

The face of marriage may be changing, but the desire to be married endures. And when people do marry again, whatever their reservations and fears, they make that decision expecting that this time it will last. For a commitment sufficient to weather the changes that will take place over the years is part of the very definition of marriage. A generation ago Anne Morrow Lindbergh defined marriage as being, by its very essence, duration and continuity. "Every relationship seems simple at its start," she wrote in *A Gift from the Sea.* "It is free of ties or claims, unburdened by responsibilities, by worry about the future or debts to the past. And then how swiftly, how inevitably the perfect unity is invaded; the relationship changes; it becomes complicated, encumbered by its contact with the world. . . . But it is the marriage relationship in which the changing pattern is shown up most clearly because it is the deepest one and the most arduous to maintain; and because, somehow, we mistakenly feel that failure to maintain its exact original pattern is tragedy. . . ."

She was describing the natural, successive stages that occur in any relationship and that are a necessary part of any good marriage: change, disruption, reconciliation, closeness and renewal. This is the great paradox that confronts anyone who marries for a second time. There is less external support to keep marriage together. We are nervous about making commitments. The marriage we enter will inevitably be evaluated primarily in the light of the relationship that is formed, yet this relationship by its very nature will change with time. Can we choose wisely? Have we learned from our previous mistakes so that we have a better chance of success? How well will we be able to handle the special stresses of a second marriage, far more complex and provocative than those of the first?

Statistics tell us that if we marry again, the odds of staying married are in the neighborhood of 60 percent. What we may not fully realize is the fact that we can improve those odds considerably by being prepared.

2

When a Marriage Ends

Every major change in life involves some degree of loss. Seldom is the loss as great as when a man or woman is widowed or goes through a divorce.

The normal response to loss is an emotional state called depression. Depression is really synonymous with grief, and because it is painful it is a mood that we would prefer to ignore or avoid. Yet a failure to recognize and know how to deal with depression is one of the greatest risks that the recently divorced or widowed person faces. Not only can it set the stage for a more enduring state of disability, one that may go on for years, but it may also set you up to make serious errors of judgment in reshaping your life once you are single again.

When people are depressed they lose perspective. You may not be able to look at the past without emphasizing your mistakes and misfortunes. You may not be able to think of the future without a sense of hopelessness and futility. You may lie awake at night or wake up early in the morning, sad and frightened. What used to matter matters less or not at all. There is an urge to withdraw from social contacts. The phone rings but goes unanswered, yet the loneliness cuts deep. Because you are slowed up and find it hard to concentrate and get things done, you must put more effort into doing what you once did spontaneously and energetically. As a result, you feel tired, anxious, tense.

Insomnia, withdrawal, a sense of desperation, at times the wish to die—these are the classical signs of depression. But rarely does this reaction appear in pure form. More often it is concealed. Depression may take the form of exquisite sensitivity; your feelings may be very easily hurt. You may feel unattractive, perhaps undeserving of love, and seriously doubt that you can ever again be cared about. Having once trusted a relationship and now feeling betrayed by life, you may wonder whether you could even give of yourself to someone else again. You may become just plain irritable, distracting yourself from the underlying depression by focusing on angry and bitter feelings toward the person you feel has wronged you.

Your reaction to loss can even be masked by a bravado that many divorced men and women display. "At last, I'm free to lead my own life." While a sense of relief may be warranted, especially when you have broken out of a debilitating relationship, the pretense at gaiety and the forced smile are often designed specifically to keep you from recognizing that the good has gone with the bad and that the future, however promising it may be, is uncertain.

With few exceptions, both partners experience the end of their marriage as a personal failure. Not infrequently this attitude may be manifested through a host of physical symptoms—headaches, stomach and intestinal pains and other vague and ill-defined complaints that defy the doctor's diagnostic acumen—to hide the true emotional state.

Mary Wentworth was forty-six, although she looked several years younger than her age, when she discovered that her husband, Frank, was seeing another woman, that he had been seeing her for some time, and, moreover, that he intended to marry her. Poking through his dresser, she had found a receipt from Eastern Airlines dated February 12, 1974, passage for two people to the island of Antigua. At first she had not recognized the symbols ANU, but a phone call to a friend in the travel business confirmed her worst fears.

When she confronted Frank with her discovery, half crying, half enraged, he denied it. Once he knew that she really knew, however, he admitted that he had spent the week with someone. He was tense and controlled as he said, "Look, Mary. We haven't much of a marriage. We haven't had for years, maybe never."

Frank slept on the couch in the living room that night. Mary didn't sleep at all. She lay there, going over and over what he had said about the marriage never having been any good. Her whole body ached. Fragmented memories flooded through her mind, all adding up to a single question: What had she done wrong?

Two recollections especially haunted her. She remembered the party in Atlanta where they first met. Walking into the room, she had noticed Frank right away. He was good-looking. Once she talked with him, she knew he was far more intriguing than most of the boys she had met. He was then a reporter for a Boston newspaper. He had traveled extensively. During the Second World War he was with the Office of Strategic Services. Mary decided then and there that this was the man she wanted to marry. Recalling now how he had been on the rebound from a love affair with a girl who had rejected him at the time and how intensely she, Mary, had pursued him made her wince.

Another scene entered her mind. They were in the living room of their small apartment in Cambridge during the first few years of their marriage. David, their son, was three. She recalled herself shouting. Frank had just returned from a trip to California. Her voice was loud and shrill as she accused him of playing around while he had been away.

Frank tried to reassure her that her suspicions were unfounded, which they were. But she would not put the accusation aside. Finally, in frustration, he walked into the bedroom and slammed the door shut. She followed, begging him to speak to her one minute, shouting at him the next. He was lying on the bed. He sat up suddenly, shook his right index finger at her and told her to "shut up." Mary grabbed it and twisted it roughly, yanking it from its socket at the knuckle. Frank was stunned. Mary fell to the floor, crying hysterically. She was as horrified remembering the incident as she had been at the time it happened.

All night long she fought the urge to go downstairs and wake Frank up and talk to him. Nor could she stop wondering whom he had taken with him to the Caribbean.

She found out two days later from her friend Karen. "I didn't want to say anything to you," said Karen, "but I've had an inkling about this for the last six months. You remember Pam? Frank used to take her out years ago, before you two married. Her husband died a couple of years ago. She moved here to Boston after that."

Mary called Frank at his office that afternoon. "Why?" she asked. He replied, "I'm fifty-two, Mary. I've found a kind of peacefulness with Pam I've never known with you. I would have left a long time ago if I hadn't been worried about the impact on you and on David. But now that David's in college and while we're both still young enough to make a new life for ourselves, I think we should call it quits."

For weeks they lived together in the same house, going about their business in silence. From time to time she would plead with him to give up Pam. He refused. He asked for a divorce. She refused. Then he moved to a hotel.

Mary felt dead inside. She tried to go about her life in her usual way, attending committee meetings, seeing friends. But she found herself crying unpredictably and at times sobbing out of control. One moment she would feel she had no future. The next she would plan ways to get back at Frank by making a scene at his office or crippling him financially. In her imagination she would call Pam up and accuse her of destroying a wonderful marriage and doing irrevocable harm to her and David. She tried once, but when Pam answered, Mary hung up. Over and over in her head she kept twisting T. S. Eliot's lines around—"That's the way a marriage ends," she thought, "not with a whimper but a bang."

One of the things that fed her resentment was the inaccurate impression that Frank, now on his own and planning to marry Pam, was happy. She could imagine him walking down a street, arm in arm with Pam, whistling, smiling.

Mary had always considered herself a strong person. "The thing to do is to stop this emotionalism," she thought, "and try to get a new life started."

She made an effort to see as many of her friends as possible as often as she could. A few months after Frank had left, however, and during the period of negotiating with lawyers, Mary began to have a variety of physical disturbances. She started to have headaches that were particularly severe in the late afternoons. She would wake up in the middle of the night with severe pains in her chest and abdomen and thought she must be developing an ulcer. Her most persistent problem was fatigue. She was tired in the mornings and by three o'clock in the afternoon so exhausted that she often had to cancel her plans for that evening and rest instead. Yet rest did little good, and the next day she would be plagued by the same round of symptoms.

Her family physician did a complete examination, including an electrocardiogram and an upper gastrointestinal series, and came up with nothing. When he suggested she might be experiencing depression, she was skeptical. When he recommended a psychiatrist, she postponed making her first appointment for nearly a month, considering the idea absurd and hoping that she would feel better. Finally, reluctantly, she followed his advice. After a couple of visits the psychiatrist gave her antidepressants. Again she refused, but a few weeks later she acquiesced, and much to her surprise she gradually began to sleep soundly without barbiturates. Her energy returned. She was less preoccupied with Frank and her ideas of revenge. Her headaches abated, and within three months she had to admit that she was feeling more like her old self than she had in years. Slowly, as she reviewed her life, she could accept the fact that, from the very beginning of the marriage, the relationship had been full of difficulties. Looking at what had happened from a different perspective, she could see that her intense jealousy, which had been so disruptive, had been rooted in an insecurity she felt living with a man who was undemonstrative and often incommunicative. "I never knew where I stood. If I would say that I loved him, he would simply smile and thank me. I liked to be with people. He hated it. I tried to show an interest in his work, but he didn't want to share it with me. For the last ten years, sex was the only thing we had in common. I don't know how or why that survived."

One of the reasons why the bewilderment and anguish that follows divorce is usually so much greater than the grief that accompanies being widowed is the fact that death frequently ends a relationship that was in many ways successful, or at least, since the other partner is not there to contradict, can be readily realigned in one's memory. It is easier to lose someone with whom you have shared years of affection than someone with whom you have known great doubt and turmoil. To know that you are cared for is, by its very nature, freeing. To live with uncertainty about whether the person you think loves you actually does, and seriously to question your own feelings about that person paradoxically intensifies the bond between the two of you. Ambivalence, as this is called, makes the termination of such a relationship far more cataclysmic.

Rarely have people who get divorced openly hated throughout most of their marriage. More often they have been linked together by a mixture of forces—love and dependency on the one hand, fear and resentment on the other. This is the kind of bond that was broken when Mary and Frank separated. The very incompatibilities that destroyed their relationship had also created a powerful interdependency between them. Mary had handled her sense of being unloved by repeatedly seeking reassurance, unsuccessfully, from him. Frank had managed his indifference to her by feeling guilty and trying to conceal his real sentiments behind a façade of responsible behavior.

When a marriage ends, everyone is demoralized. No matter how bad the situation has been, there is no way to avoid the feeling that someone you thought loved you no longer does. How can you not feel that you have failed somehow to make it work, or at least that you made a serious error in judgment when you chose to marry? In either case, a long shadow will cast itself over your self-esteem for some time to come.

Many marriages that end in divorce reveal a long history of poor communication. You or your partner may not have been able to set intelligent limits on intrusions or domination by the other, or conflicts were never voiced, only to remain, simmering, beneath the surface, and giving rise to resentments that were neither expressed nor resolved. Many people cannot directly recognize, experience, and deal with angry feelings and, as a result, become depressed instead. As one woman, in her late thirties, put it, "I lived with my husband for fifteen years, and in all that time I don't think I raised my voice to him once. He wasn't an abusive or unkind man. But he was very insensitive in countless small ways. He wouldn't hesitate, for instance, to call at ten of seven, when dinner had been planned for seven, to tell me he wouldn't be home until later. And often he'd just not call at all, but he'd always have some legitimate excuse that related to his work. On birthdays or for Christmas he was generous with money, but he'd never bother to get me or even any of the children a gift he had picked out himself.

"After we were divorced—I won't go into the details now—I felt so awful I had to see a therapist. It was only then that I could recognize how much downright anger I had stored up, by never telling him how I felt, and how these emotions were pulling me deeper and deeper into a state of depression."

The more dependent you are on the person to whom you have been married as well as on the state of marriage itself—children, home, a way of life, your image of yourself—the more vulnerable you will be to being depressed if it fails. Bill and Janet Parker had been married for only six years when they were divorced. Bill was a physician. He was a lanky, attractive man who looked somewhat like a young Henry Fonda. He had met Janet when they were both undergraduates at the University of Virginia. Three years later, when Bill was a second-year medical student at Johns Hopkins, they were married.

Janet continued her studies to become an architect and worked for another three years until their daughter, Evan, was born. Meanwhile, Bill completed his internship and went on to begin a residency in internal medicine at Hopkins. These were good years for them. The only factor that marred their life was the stress imposed by Janet's mother, an alcoholic. Periodically, she would create a crisis to which Janet and Bill always responded, hospitalizing her, drying her out, urging her to join Alcoholics Anonymous. Janet's father had long since departed for places unknown.

One evening, as they were entertaining a group of friends from the hospital, dinner was interrupted by a telephone call. The policeman on the other end informed Janet that her mother had been in an automobile accident. She was intoxicated at the time. Drifting through a stop sign without pausing, she had been struck by a large trailer truck. After hitting her car, the truck careened across the highway, striking a station wagon. The wagon exploded and the woman and two children in it were killed. Janet's mother was in critical condition. Three days later she was dead.

Janet went through the funeral without showing a trace of emotion. She was prepared for such a tragedy and seemed able to cope with it. Bill tried to be supportive. Neither could shake the sense of guilt about the children who had been the innocent victims of the accident. They asked themselves whether they should have been more active in dealing with Janet's mother and her problem.

As the next few months passed, Janet's personality seemed to change. She drew more and more into herself and did not want to see friends. She continued her work but was extremely tired at night and in bed by nine o'clock. When Bill made any sexual advances, she would put him off without explanation. On several occasions, when he came home for dinner, he found her half asleep on the bed, intoxicated. She began to punctuate their conversations with sarcasm and accuse Bill of being inconsiderate, interested only in himself, and of giving her no room in which to breathe.

At first, Bill was angry and bewildered by Janet's behavior and warned her to stop drinking lest she become like her mother. In calmer moments he would ask her to talk with him about her feelings. She would not. When he raised the possibility of her seeing a psychiatrist, she countered with "You see one! You're the problem!"

As Janet shut Bill out more and more, he grew increasingly anxious. No longer could he be at all objective. He knew that Janet's behavior had been triggered by the accident, but he couldn't convince her of this, and as his own helplessness and frustration mounted he grew quite depressed. He had always been dependent on his wife, in a complex way that went far beyond the ordinary details of running a home. She had been the first girl he had ever been in love with. He had always doubted his appeal for women, and when Janet, who was quite attractive and popular, seemed interested in him, this completely removed his uncertainty. Moreover, the security he found in the relationship with her extended to every other aspect of his life as well. His grades improved. He felt more at ease socially.

He was especially proud of his marriage and his family.

He carried a picture of Janet and Evan in his wallet and kept another on his desk. He would never go to any school or hospital parties without her. Now, faced with her rejection of him, he gradually fell apart. "Please, Janet, please," he said one evening shortly after arriving home. "I can't stand this any more. I can't function without you. If this keeps up, I won't be able to go on working. You've got to do something. Marriage counseling. Anything." Janet thought a minute, then replied, "I can't help it if you're weak. I have to use all the energy I have to keep myself together. I'm not sure I love you any more, Bill. Maybe if we live apart for a while you can gain some strength and so can I."

"Is there someone else?" Bill asked.

"No."

"How do I know?"

"You don't. You'll just have to take my word for it." Bill moved to the residents' quarters at the hospital. Alone, frightened, he missed Janet terribly. He missed Evan and their life together. All he looked ahead to was taking Evan to the park or the zoo on weekends. It was invariably painful to bring her home again and say goodbye. Janet always managed to be out at those times.

Christmas Eve, following their separation, he returned Evan after dinner and then went back to his room and cried for half an hour. After that he went out to a singles bar, drank three whiskey sours, picked up a girl and went home with her. Christmas morning, waking up in a strange place, he felt sick. He went to the bathroom and threw up. Then, while the girl was still sleeping, he dressed, went down to the railroad station, and took the Amtrak to Philadelphia for Christmas dinner with his parents.

Bill continued to live in the house staff quarters for several months. At first he didn't care about the fact that it was grim, sterile, and lonely. Most of the interns and other staff members used those rooms only when they were on call. The walls were painted a decrepit yellow, with cheap prints hanging on them and a hospital blanket on the bed. As a rule he ate dinner in the cafeteria. His appetite was poor and he lost ten pounds, making his already thin frame look gaunt. He found himself from time to time thinking about suicide as a possibility, and during these periods especially his medical work afforded him valuable distraction.

One of his close friends told Bill that he had better do something for himself or he'd collapse entirely. Fortunately, he listened. He began to attend a weekly group discussion for recently divorced people. Here he received a good deal of encouragement. "A lot of people behave irrationally when they're depressed" and "you're young and have your whole life in front of you" and "you can still be a good father" and "you'd better get out of that depressing place you're living in" were some of the suggestions that caught his attention. He found a more cheerful place to live. He gradually discovered that his real problem was that he had never really become self-sufficient. This deficit had been well concealed behind his white clinic coat and the authority he had at work. In his personal life, however, he had never allowed himself to become really independent. He had lived at home with his family until college. Once having become involved with Janet, he felt that he could never again meet anyone with whom he could have a significant relationship; that was one of the reasons, however fragile, that he had married her to begin with. It also explained why, walking down the street, he would experience a sharp twinge of futility and envy when he would see a man and a woman hand in hand.

It was time for him to explore life more actively and

learn to be more assertive. As much as he wanted to see Janet and talk with her, he found that the few times he did he only came away feeling quite low. About eight months after their break-up he had to attend a medical conference in Denver. Sitting on the plane, he noticed a pretty young flight attendant. With considerable self-consciousness and trepidation, he wrote her a note, asking her if she would like to have a drink with him. In his imagination he thought she might just open the note, show it to one of the other attendants or crew members, and be amused. He was surprised, then, when she came back to where he was seated and politely accepted. Although he never saw her again, this minor turning point helped him establish confidence in his relationship with women.

When your marriage ends, it is perfectly natural for you to feel at least some degree of depression. If you can recognize this mood, you will be able to take the first steps toward relieving your distress. But all too often, because we just don't know what signs to look for, we miss seeing the whole picture. And so we run the risk of dealing with each separate symptom in a haphazard and ultimately unsuccessful way.

Your marriage is over. Are you now going through what is a basically normal process of grief? To find out, you can ask yourself the following set of questions. The more times your answer is "yes," the more likely you are to be experiencing depression.

Do you have chronic trouble sleeping? Even when you fall asleep easily, do you wake up early in the morning unable to go back to sleep again, bothered by feelings of nervousness, sadness, fear, or a general reluctance to face the day ahead?

Is it hard to clear your mind of the issues and problems that upset you? Do you find yourself dwelling on hurts or grievances, going over and over again in circles your concerns about your future, usually with a sense of futility?

Do you feel painful moments of loneliness?

Is your self-esteem shattered? Do you feel older than your years, unattractive, sexually undesirable and generally ineffectual as a person? Are you haunted by a sense of failure? Guilt?

What's happened to your sexual drive? Has it disappeared? Or is it unusually intense? What about your weight? Are you eating too much or has your appetite fallen off, so that you have lost ten pounds or more without trying?

Do you feel rejected? Do other people seem unusually critical of you? Do you assume that when your telephone is silent it means people are avoiding you?

Or are you avoiding people, feeling too tired, listless, unmotivated or afraid to see friends and family, withdrawing more and more into yourself?

Have you lost interest in the things that used to stimulate you? Do you find it hard to concentrate enough to read or pay attention to your work?

Or maybe you feel unusually cheerful, throwing caution to the wind, spending more money than you should on things you don't need. Have you an urge to throw everything over, suddenly, impatiently, quit your job, sell your house, move to some other part of the country?

Having been in pretty good health, do you now find yourself subject to a variety of physical complaints—stomach pains, headaches, fatigue—that keep you running to the doctor or the drug store in a vain search for relief?

What's happened to your temper? Is it hard to feel angry? Or have you instead suddenly become more irritable and impatient than you used to be?

If you see yourself in several of these descriptions, it simply means that you are experiencing the usual changes that go along with being depressed. It does not mean that you are going out of your mind. These reactions are the natural ones to a serious and traumatic loss and should be recognized as such. Once you know you are in a state of depression you can create strategies to deal with the helplessness and special vulnerability that it can induce. For example, you will realize the good sense of putting off major decisions while you are in such a state, in taking care not to complicate your life any further. It is important to avoid behavior that will only serve to reinforce your lowered sense of self-esteem, such as alcohol to block out the pain temporarily or ill-advised sexual or romantic liaisons sought out to reassure you that you are still desirable, or impulsive and poorly thought-through changes in your career motivated by a desire to escape from yourself.

How well you can cope with depression and how effectively you can recover from it depends partly on the kind of person you are. The more flexible and resourceful you can be, the more quickly you can overcome its effects. How you regard your emotional state is critical. If you look on your condition as a sign of weakness or an abnormality, or if you are guided in your actions by your pessimism, you will certainly aggravate it and make the mood last longer. Denying its presence can have the same consequence. If, on the other hand, you regard depression as a normal reaction to the kind of stress you've been through, you won't be frightened by it and you will be able to let it gradually disappear.

Here are several other constructive measures you can use to help deal with this emotional state and overcome it:

Simple as it sounds, get as much rest as you can. You

will find that sleep is therapeutic. On the other hand, do not turn to alcohol or sleeping pills as a solution. The more you depend on natural methods to sleep—warm milk at night, a warm bath, avoiding too much stimulation just before retiring—the better.

Rest, however, is only part of the solution. Activity is also an antidote for depression. The important thing is to choose things to do that you want to do, enjoy doing, and that you are able to do. If you can't concentrate well enough to read, try working with your hands. Dig in the garden. Knit. Bowl. Go to a film. Play cards. Activity will give you the kind of satisfaction that takes the edge off the feelings of inadequacy, helping to restore your self-confidence.

Don't expect too much of yourself. These will not be your most productive or creative days. If you have critical choices to make and can postpone them until your perspective returns, do so. If you are fortunate enough to be working in an environment where you can be open and frank, let your colleagues know you are under pressure so they do not misinterpret your waning performance, tendency to put things off, or touchiness as something other than it is.

Spend time with people, primarily those with whom you feel comfortable. Some of these will be close friends in whom you can confide, and most of them will help to distract you from thinking too much about yourself and your predicament. Avoid those who stir you up, who irritate sensitive nerves and make you feel resentful or more hopeless than you already do.

Remember, you are not alone. At one time or another every one of us faces some serious disruption in his or her life, often unexpectedly, usually compromising our self-esteem. Right now you may feel like a failure. But success is not "making it"; it is being able to pick yourself up after a major defeat and rebuild your life from that point on.

It is always a sound idea to consider professional counseling of some kind. Not only will this provide you with an objective and experienced person who can help you think about your future more clearly, but for many, such as Mary Wentworth, it permits an evaluation for the use of antidepressant medications. Stress affects everyone physically as well as psychologically. It is frequently difficult to reverse the physical changes that accompany depression, even when you have taken definitive steps to change yourself or improve your life situation. The judicious use of tricyclic antidepressants can accelerate the process of recovery.

Nor should you hesitate to seek professional help because you assume that it will involve lengthy analysis. It usually does not. To share your experiences and feelings with someone who can be objective and is trustworthy has many advantages over just turning to friends, who may tend to see your life through your eyes or their own and may encourage you to blame your former husband or wife exclusively for what has happened. Dissolving the bond is a complex task and often requires an expertise that is not available through haphazard or amateurish forms of therapy.

It is, in fact, advisable to consult someone in most instances, however briefly and however mild your depressive mood may be, even though this runs counter to a general assumption that it is better to deal with your moods on your own. It is unfortunate that many people, to their own detriment, will reject out of hand the suggestion to seek expert advice, just to prove they are truly independent.

Finally, as difficult as it may be, try to view what seems like a disaster as an opportunity. This is obviously easier to do if divorce has freed you from an intolerable situation. It is harder, of course, when something that seemed positive has been taken away. Without underestimating the tragedy that the end of a marriage often represents, you now have a good chance to evaluate seriously what went wrong, to consider the kind of person you have been and want to become, and to plan the sort of life you wish to build for yourself in the years to come.

3

Outdistancing Our Shadows

In *Brideshead Revisited,* novelist Evelyn Waugh wrote: "We get bourne along, out of sight in the press, unresisting, till we get the chance to drop behind unnoticed, or to dodge down a side street, pause, breathe freely and take our bearing, or to push ahead, outdistance our shadows, lead them a dance, so that when at length they catch up with us, they look at one another askance, knowing we have a secret we shall never share."

Being single again is a chance to do just that. We can drop behind or push ahead and rethink what has been counterfeit and what has been real. As we rearrange the details of our lives, attending to such matters as where to live, how to establish new relationships, what to do with the children when they visit, and how to mold the character of our contact with former husbands and wives, we now have a unique opportunity to reappraise ourselves by examining the past and planning the future.

One basic issue that emerges is existential in character. Every man and woman is ultimately alone. At some point in life, in order truly to live, we must face the full implications of that aloneness. For years we have been going to lengths to avoid facing it. Living on top of one another, crowding in, going where everyone else goes, surrounding ourselves with things or causes, accumulating symbols of success—all these devices have been employed to deny this central truth, including marriage itself.

Dr. Bill Parker had to recognize this when he acknowledged his lack of self-sufficiency. Throughout his life he had depended on some kind of external structure—his family, his work, Janet—to get his bearings. As he learned to live alone, he had to resist the temptation to prematurely lock himself into either his work or his new relationships with women in order to permit a healthy sense of autonomy to evolve. He also found that putting some distance between himself and his familiar surroundings helped.

"After Janet and I had been divorced for nearly a year, I took some savings and traveled for three months in Europe. I had just finished my training and had not yet decided what to do next. As the weeks went by, my past life seemed more and more remote. You know how you look back, years later, on something like high school or college that seemed like a really long time when you were going through it and how, later, it seems like a brief flash in time, years pressed into minutes? Well, it was like that. Sometimes I didn't even feel like me. I had absorbed so much of my identity from my marriage and work that when I stopped to consider it, I had lost touch with myself.

"I was still hung up on Janet. I was still convinced that I would never find anyone else, in spite of my gestures toward meeting new girls. Everyone told me I was crazy. I knew they were right. But it didn't make any difference. I was convinced that I could never fall in love again.

"In Rome I met this girl. She was French. We saw a lot of each other. It was only a week. She was twenty-seven, bright, intuitive. We had to communicate in three languages, a little French, some Italian, and some English, since I didn't speak any foreign language well. One evening, walking through the ruins of the Colosseum after the light-and-sound show had finished, I was talking about Janet. She took my hand. Squeezing it tightly, she said, "The world is full of women." For some strange reason, in that place, from that girl, thousands of miles removed from everyday life, what she said registered with me for the first time, and I began to feel freer, more hopeful."

Distancing is one of the more effective methods to stimulate creative thinking. We are all encumbered by biases and assumptions, the residues of our past lives that we acquire, like barnacles, from childhood on. These premises seriously influence how we perceive ourselves and our lives. Stripping away the structure that marriage has provided can set the stage to free us from the control of some of these premises, such as "There is only one girl for me" or "I cannot function without him." Introducing some space—geographical, the passage of time—between ourselves and our lives catalyzes this process.

The major challenge that confronts the newly divorced or widowed person is to think and act creatively. Creativity, after all, is nothing more or less than the ability to see things in a fresh and different way. Hence, it is a function of the personality that is especially necessary to reconstruct your life after a major change has occurred. And if you are recently divorced or widowed, the multiple uncertainties of your life can seem overwhelming. In an unfamiliar situation you must move forward toward an unclear future. This requires some imagination on your part, and there is no better time to learn and practice some creative thinking.

However elusive the concept of creativity may appear, extensive analyses of the creative process have all found that it consists of four basic stages: preparation, incubation, illumination, and verification.

The first stage is *preparation*. This is when you gather all the information and experience you need to lead you to some new ideas. If, for instance, you are going to take advantage of your new situation to find a different kind of career or occupation, you should familiarize yourself with the options realistically available. You obviously have to fit your experience and credentials to the needs of the labor market.

But at the same time and even more importantly, you should explore yourself. The things we do best and from which we derive our greatest satisfaction are often those which most closely suit our talents and temperament. How can we find them? Ask yourself:

What did you like to do as a child, especially as an adolescent? After the busy, fast-flowing years since—those dedicated to making a living, raising a family, struggling with conflicts—what old and neglected interests can you revitalize?

If you could create any kind of daily routine that you wished, what would it be like? Would you prefer a regular, predictable sort of life or one that is not?

Would you prefer to work with things or with people? Indoors or outdoors? Within the security of an organization, large or small, or on your own? Do you like immediate results or can you wait?

The answers to such questions as these will clue you into your basic interest patterns. From these you will be able to identify the ones which fit into the framework of current possibilities.

To come up with good ideas, however, you will have to observe one of the fundamental rules for creative thinking: *quantity equals quality*. The more ideas you come up with, the greater your chances of hitting on some that are original and particularly suited to your present needs. Our normal tendency is to find one or two solutions and stop there. If they work, fine. If not, we feel blocked and futile again. The point is keep the flow of ideas going, allowing, as well, those that seem silly or even absurd. If you keep on and add as many more ideas as you can think of, you will eventually come upon a few that are truly original, exciting, and begin to make sense to you.

Or you may still come up with no satisfactory answers. And this leads us to the next stage in the creative process: *incubation*. Our unconscious is the source of our creative ideas. Ordinary logical thought often arrives only at those solutions that we already know and that have already failed to work. Within the unconscious, out of sight, however, our minds can work at whirlwind speed, putting together ideas in combinations that defy logic, drawing on memories of experiences that have long since been forgotten in order to offer us possibilities that we could never have thought of otherwise.

Incubation takes time. Hours, weeks, even months may be required, depending on the complexity of the issues. Dwelling on your problems will usually delay resolution. What you have to learn to do is put them aside for a while and let them simmer.

Simmering will set you up for the third stage in the creative process: *illumination*. At some unexpected moment, walking on the beach, lying in bed at night, in the middle of a conversation with a friend, ideas begin to flash into your mind. Good ideas. Ideas that just might work. And at this point it is important to apply the second cardinal rule of creative thinking: *the principle of deferred judgment.*

Most of us pass judgment on our ideas as soon as they occur to us. "I would like to get a job," you say. But right away, something whispers: "You can't. You haven't worked for years. No one will hire you. You don't have the right academic degrees or skills." You would like to meet a new man with whom you can form a close relationship, maybe even marry. That voice inside shouts: "You're too old. Besides, all the interesting men are already married." Or it says: "Marriage is for fools." You'd like to marry again and have more children, but "who would want a man of forty who has to support an ex-wife and three kids in school?"

These criticisms reflect the "it won't work" philosophy that causes most of us to fail to arrive at original ideas by killing them off before they have had a chance to materialize. And while other people also tend to put our ideas down, we are usually our own worst, most negative enemies.

So, save your more realistic, analytic weighing of the value of your options until the fourth and final stage in the creative process: *verification.* You'll need it then. This is when you find out, for example, whether the talent and interest you have is marketable and then learn how to go about marketing it. This is when you start dating desirable women, for example, and find out whether you are likely to be rejected as a loser or held in higher esteem than you may have been holding yourself. Or this is when you begin to define for yourself just what kind of sexual involvements, if any, you intend to engage in with the various men you go out with.

Gaining insight into yourself—trying to figure out what you want of the future and examining the past for clues about what may have gone wrong in your former marriage—is itself a creative experience. To discover, for example, that you have continued to be very attached to your former spouse and that this very attachment is the root of the resentment, disguised in the form of blame, that you continue to feel toward him or her, is a creative act. Then, to let go—to really let go—of such feelings so that you can move forward to build a life of your own is precisely the kind of personal change that can be accomplished only through creativity.

One important guideline for the newly divorced man or woman to follow in reconstructing his or her life is: Expose yourself to as many different ideas and situations as you can and do so actively.

Another important strategy that is quite effective in promoting original solutions is to *restate the problem* that you face. Money is almost always a problem after divorce. There is seldom a way in which people can live better apart, except perhaps when each is entitled to Social Security payments. The tax bracket is higher for each. The burden may be eased if the woman works, if she is not already working. But divorce commonly destroys the family's economic security. Alimony is tax deductible, at least, but child support is not and is rarely enough anyway. Moreover, a family's financial planning has usually been done on the assumption that husband and wife will stay together and is shattered when they break up.

It is best to accept the fact that there will be a change in the standard of living, for a while at least, unless one can find a way to make more money. For the man, in particular, there may be less freedom rather than more. If he wants to be near his children and see them with any frequency, he may lose some of the mobility that is often required for job advancement. If they live in Los Angeles, he may no longer be free to take a job in Chicago that might further his career and that he probably would have taken had the family remained intact.

Many people unwisely preoccupy themselves with the issue of how they can continue to live in the style to which they have grown accustomed. How can they go on doing what they have been doing in spite of the altered circumstances? Far better to ask the question: "If I had no past to compare my life with, what sort of style would suit me best now?" Often the answer is quite unexpected.

Carolyn Chambers was forty-two years old when she was divorced. She and her former husband had been living in a four-bedroom suburban house in Kansas City's Garden District. They had originally purchased it for sixty-five thousand dollars and it was now worth close to a hundred and twenty-five thousand. They had joint ownership and agreed to sell it.

Carolyn looked around at other houses and some apartments to find a suitable replacement, but she was discouraged by the prices. At the same time, she was painfully reluctant to move to a neighborhood that would reflect the shift downward in her economic status. They had belonged to a very socially conscious group and she knew that, even if no one mentioned it to her, the friends that she had would quietly be talking about her and feeling sorry for her.

Gradually she started to appreciate the freedom that her present situation offered. There was no reason why she should stay in Kansas City at all. There was no reason why her children should continue in private schools at high cost. She herself was not geared to a highly competitive career and did not want to work at a job that she found uninteresting or unpleasant, just for the money.

So she asked herself: What kind of life might best suit me now? Where have I been the happiest?

In the summers the family had vactioned on Cape Cod. Hyannis was a growing city. The schools were good. The cost of living, while not cheap, was below that of her present situation. She was an outgoing person and knew that she would have little trouble meeting new people. For years she had thought it would be enjoyable to work in a retail shop, a dress boutique or a card-and-gift shop. She already had quite a few friends who also spent time on the Cape. Some were moving there to live year round. Nor was the Cape so inaccessible that her husband could not come to visit their three children periodically and perhaps spend time in the summers. So, after some exploration, she bought a small house there and began a new life, one that she could not only afford but could not afford to pass by.

If you ask the wrong questions, you will inevitably come up with wrong answers. Restating the issues, as Carolyn did, is one way to avoid the trap of perpetuating the economic resentments that so commonly accompany divorce. In this way, one can begin to think of constructive alternatives to seeking out lawyers to sue ex-husbands for more money and other lawyers to calculate how to cut down on the money a husband is obligated to give for the support of his former family.

Carolyn was also observing another valuable tenet—namely, to establish yourself in a new life, if possible, before taking on the responsibilities of another marriage. Systems theory, which has become quite popular in behavioral sciences in recent years, emphasizes that we can understand ourselves only by understanding our relationships with those around us and that each set of relationships has its own character. Each of us is the center of his or her own little universe. But we are circling planets in someone else's universe and perhaps only a burned-out star in yet another's. The balance of forces among people is such that whatever happens to one individual in the system affects everyone else and changes the very character of the system itself. The closer to the center of the group you are, the more of an impact you will produce—or feel—when any significant change occurs.

The end of a marriage is the end of a system, or world. It is like an explosion that sends you rocketing off into space, weightless, without attachments or the secure pull of a predictable orbit. Here and there floats the residual debris from your former world. But essentially, for a while, you drift freely.

Gradually a new system is formed. A different way of life is set up that involves many people, some from the past, some from the present, all of whom begin to fall into place in a new equilibrium. There are the men and women you date, the children of your former marriage who come to expect certain things of you and you of them, now, outside the context of family life as it was.

"I was thirty-seven when we were divorced, and now, looking back nearly ten years, I can see what a profound change I went through at that time, in every way." Bob Petree was an attorney with a law firm in New York. A very religious man, he had never expected his marriage to fall apart, and when it did it took him nearly a year to recover from the emotional and moral dilemma that the event created for him.

"To begin with, I was Catholic. I had to face squarely the question of whether I could ever marry again, or even date for that matter. I had gone to Catholic schools. In fact, I had attended Mass nearly every day for years. Then, suddenly, I had to decide for myself what my moral obligations were to myself and my children and even to my former wife. I decided that I had to start building a new and full life and that I might have to forfeit formal religion in favor of a more personal sense of God."

Bob had four children, two boys and two girls. The youngest was four, the oldest thirteen. "Their mother had custody, and I had the right to see them every other weekend, and I did. I'd take them Friday night and bring them back Sunday. The oldest child, Debbie, was really upset about the divorce, and so was my ten-year-old son, Sam. I felt it was important to give them as much support as I could so they wouldn't think that I might disappear from their lives."

As the initial turbulence settled, he noticed a change in the nature of his relationship with his children. When he and his wife had been living together, she had pretty much managed the affairs at home by herself and by her own choice. He was left to pursue his career. She picked the schools the children attended, decided about such matters as summer camp and birthday parties and presents at Christmas. Bob more or less went along with this. By nature, his wife was quite a forceful person, and over the years he had deferred to her need to control their social life and the character of their home.

"I am convinced that ultimately the children benefitted from the divorce. I could never really be myself within the marriage. I didn't try. I didn't even consider it a problem at the time. Alone, on my own, I emerged as a person with them. Not just doing things together and not just the personal relationships, but I stepped out of the shadows and they could see their father as an individual rather than a blur."

Over years of marriage you can easily lose touch with the person you once were before marriage. And being alone again often stimulates a rebirth of old traits and highly personal interest patterns. As with many men, Bob Petree had abdicated the selection of friends to his wife, who, in turn, had inadvertently but systematically removed him from many of the friends he had known in college and law school. Although he had not spoken with some of them in years and was not without embarrassment and some fear that if he called them he would be greeted coolly, Bob nonetheless contacted a number of his old friends and found the welcome warm. "If I ever marry again," he thought, "I won't make the mistake of letting these friendships die again."

He also made some radical changes in his career direction as well. When he decided to attend law school, it had not been an easy choice. There were many other things that he wanted to do as well. He had considered journalism, teaching, a business career, preferably in publishing. In his school days he had been quite active in debating, dramatics, and student government. Because of his high grades, when he graduated from Yale Law School he was offered a number of excellent opportunities and accepted a position with his present firm. He made partner within seven years. At first, handling large corporate clients appealed to him, but as time went on he grew bored with the years of effort necessary to negotiate some merger or resolve some tax dispute and he wearied of the endless nights spent at the printer's, going over the wording in page after page of legal documents. From time to time he expressed a desire to find a different kind of practice, but his wife reminded him to be proud of his accomplishments and not jeopardize their financial success by taking any unnecessary risks. As usual, he acquiesced.

Single again, his dissatisfaction with the work he was doing grew. Instinctively he began to compare the nature of his current daily activities with the kind of life he had enjoyed years before. He liked variety. He liked dealing with people more than paperwork. He liked the world of publishing and communications. His present position, even though it rewarded him well, provided none of these opportunities.

"I tried to figure out how I wanted to spend each day, and the answer I came up with was a far cry from what I was doing. I decided the thing to do was to talk with people. So I went back to Yale and spoke to a few of my old teachers, and I talked with lawyer friends over lunch and some writers I knew and publishers. The outcome of this search was an opportunity to join a fine, small firm that specialized in copyright law and I took it. That was six years ago. I make a good living, by no means as much as I would have made if I had stayed in the corporate area, but enough, and I look ahead to what I'm doing every day, so much so that the years rush by. Funny thing, when I resigned my partnership everyone in the old firm thought I must be leaving for the West Coast or quitting the profession or just out of my mind. It made absolutely no sense to them at all."

Within four years, Bob Petree's world bore little resemblance to the world he had once inhabited. The fact that he had taken up skiing, began to wear suits from Dunhill Tailors, and decorated his apartment with his own photography was only the external sign of an inner change. The most important aspect of that inner change was his ability to define himself. It was Martin Buber who proposed the I-Thou concept, and after the We of being married has ended, a new I has to be created before one can commit oneself to another marriage. Bob Petree did just that.

One of the fundamental rules to follow during this period of reconstruction is to be open to change and to allow events to evolve. Swiss psychiatrist Carl Jung postulated a theory of synchronicity. Things that seem to happen by chance have a profound influence on the course of our lives and may well be operating according to laws of nature that we cannot, in our present state of knowledge, comprehend. A successful life is often the result of the proper balance between self-determination and cooperation with events over which we have no obvious control and generally attribute to fate. Hence it is often a serious mistake to attempt to force things and better to move with events as long as they represent a clearly positive route that seems to be leading somewhere.

Nowhere is this creative principle as important to the divorced or widowed individual as in the formation of new romantic attachments, one of which may lead to another marriage.

4

The Search for Someone Else

Few remedies are more effective for restoring self-esteem after a marriage fails than to find another man or woman to care about who cares about you. Such a relationship also gives you an opportunity to learn how to trust your feelings again and regain confidence in your own ability to love.

Formerly married people have a decided advantage in a culture as tolerant as ours has become. With greater freedom from a number of old social restraints, you can more easily explore new relationships actively and with varying degrees of involvement. You can live with someone, if you choose, for a year, for example, and still call it off if things don't work out. It may be hard for some to recall nowadays, and difficult to imagine for those who were not dating then, that there was a time when serious emotional involvements were automatically expected to lead to marriage. More than a few first marriages were injudiciously made because a woman felt she had to marry the man with whom she had had her first complete sexual experience. Many marriages occurred because a man felt trapped by a sense of obligation into offering a woman a lasting commitment. Guilt and one's public image rather than good sense often led to unfortunate unions.

In some ways, however, we have gone to the opposite extreme. This is the age of instant coffee, instant banking, instant closeness and instant sex, all of which makes it difficult to allow enough time to pass to establish a genuinely meaningful relationship. As one forty-year-old man described: "I remember taking out this attractive woman after a party. When we got to her house, she asked me to come in for a drink. I was tired and had an important meeting the next day, so I asked for a rain check. The next time I saw her we went to a ball game and back to my place for a cookout. When the evening was over, I drove her home. Just before she got out of the car, she looked at me in a puzzled way and asked, 'Are you okay?' 'What do you mean?' She replied, 'Don't you like women?' I was astonished. 'What ever made you think that?' 'This is our second time out together and you haven't even made a pass at me.' "

Each relationship that you form should be valued for its own sake. A mistake many men and women make is to think that every new person they meet or become acquainted with should be considered a possible means of reentering marriage. Finding someone to marry can become such a strong point of reference that you view each person who comes along in those terms. Then, should there be something about that person that makes them seem unsuited for marriage to you, the relationship is never given a chance to evolve.

Mary Wentworth found herself in that position. She began to see a good deal of a fifty-one-year-old widower who was quite devoted to her. But because she had made up her mind not to marry him, she felt hemmed in by his attention and at times even thought of him with disdain: "He's too dependent on me. I don't like the feeling of being in control. That's what happened in my first marriage. This man is a lot more empathetic than my former husband. When I'm upset, he knows how to make me feel better. He's gentle, kind. It's hard to fault him. But when he sends me flowers, instead of being happy I get irritated. I constantly feel the need to set limits on him to remind him I'm not interested in marriage. I've even refused to see him for weeks at a time." Only when Mary stopped evaluating her relationship with reference to its marriage possibilities could she relax and enjoy it for the friendship it was.

A similar problem was evident in the behavior of a thirty-four-year-old divorced man who, rather than being open to meeting new women, only wanted to find a woman with whom he could have a really "meaningful" relationship. "I wasn't interested in anyone unless I knew that we would, almost from the very beginning, become something special to each other. If the girl didn't look right or have the right set of interests, I wouldn't pursue it further."

On one occasion a couple he had known for years invited him to visit them in Washington for a weekend. They arranged to introduce him to a dozen or so unattached women. There was a cocktail party Friday night, followed by dinner, and he met more of their friends at breakfast the next day, lunch, tea, drinks, and dinner, and on Sunday they followed a similar routine. "It was like a military campaign. By the end of the weekend I was exhausted. I kept hoping I'd meet that special person, and I'd turn off the minute something wasn't quite right. I recall one woman who was attractive and interesting enough. She was about thirty. I think we could have become good friends. But she had a son around nine, and I'd already made up my mind I didn't want to marry someone with children. So I just never called her again."

Marriage on the mind is a real deterrent to the kind of exploration necessary to making a good adjustment to the single life and preparing for another marriage. Similarly, if you are preoccupied by a need to form a romantically exciting relationship, feeling miserable without one, you will do yourself a disservice. For you will most likely overlook the very things you might otherwise gain from friendships with people of the opposite sex—someone to confide in, learn from, share with. You may bypass some excellent chances to know people well worth knowing, and as you move in and out of relationships in search of an ideal one, you will probably multiply unnecessarily the opportunities to be unhappy and lonely as you go through each new ending.

Memory is clever at playing tricks. Even though one marriage has ended disastrously, many people find it hard to acknowledge that the formal marriage contract is no guarantee of endurance. They want the security and permanence that marriage once seemed to insure, ignoring the fact that, especially in this society, valuing a relationship for its own sake may well be the best way to protect its survival. Respect is critical, and if a man and woman's relationship is rooted in respect for each other, their closeness can last even if one or the other marries someone else. "Some of the men I went out with are still my good friends," observed one remarried woman. "There's nothing of an intimate nature between us. My new husband likes them, accepts them without jealousy, and I am certainly not indiscreet with regard to how I handle these relationships now."

While a few may be fortunate enough to come upon a special romantic relationship rapidly, most people do not. Narrowing the field too soon is a common error.

You should really get to know a number of different people before making any final decisions about marrying again. This can be a special problem for those of you who were originally married at a young age, remained married for some time, and were relatively faithful throughout. You may have grown accustomed to forming only one emotional involvement at a time. You find it hard to think of caring for more than one person simultaneously. Once you are close to a person, you may begin to experience a sense of loyalty that deters you from being open to seeing someone else. It is a variation on the theme of fidelity, but, since the kind of commitment that is part of being married is not called for, it is usually quite inappropriate. It can be a dangerous trap that often prevents the exploration of legitimate options that may be within ready reach and vital for your personal development. "I dated one girl for four months," commented one man. "Then I met another and was attracted to her. That made me feel guilty toward both of them. I kept feeling I had to choose between them. In fact, under the circumstances, such a choice was quite irrelevant."

Establishing a number of relationships during this period of reconstruction is important since, among other things, it is a time to learn. For some men, such as Bob Petree, who had very little experience with women before his marriage, it represented a second chance to do what he should have done in his adolescence and early twenties—namely, test himself out in a variety of situations in order to better understand the notion of compatibility. Had he done so, it is unlikely that he would have married the woman he did.

His wife was the first girl he had dated regularly. She was basically a self-centered person, ungiving and unable to express herself on any subject without overtones of brittle sarcasm. As a result, Bob did not know what it was to have a relationship with a woman that involved sharing and communicating directly.

During the two years after his divorce, he went out with several different women. "It's hard to put into words," he said, "but it was only as I got to know Robin that I began to realize how skewed everything had been with my wife. It may sound foolish, but for instance I'd say to my wife something like 'What did you do today?' and she would answer by throwing the same question back at me—'What did you do today?'—and adding an ugly inflection. I'd ask her about her family, how her father was, and she'd come back with 'What's the point in asking? You can't stand him anyway', which just wasn't true. I was always being put on the defensive, and if I wanted to discuss something at work, she'd sit there, watching television, telling me not to interrupt her.

"Robin came as a shock. The words flowed between us. It was startling to get a direct answer to a question or to be asked what kind of day I had had or to be able to think out loud and not run into some kind of critical remark."

Robin was a very pleasant person whose general good humor was interrupted from time to time by her quick temper. She could not stand lateness. Once, when Bob was delayed for an hour she was furious with him. It actually scared him at first, but as he grew more familiar with her temperament, he noticed important differences between her reactions and those of his former wife. Robin might shout about his being late, but her outbursts were never scathing, never an attack on him as a person. She often apologized afterward. She did not harbor resentment and bring the issue up again and again. When it was over, it was over. As he felt more secure with her, he was able to become angry himself occasionally when it was warranted.

Bob Petree also learned, gradually, the paradox with which the single person must cope. Only when you are prepared not to marry again can you even consider remarriage. The option of remaining single must be felt as a legitimate alternative. You can commit yourself to a new marriage only when you are free not to.

Going out with a number of different women, some his own age, some younger, a few older, Bob Petree gained another important insight. In each relationship he was different. Some brought out the best in him, some the worst. Moreover, each involvement had its own special character. Gradually he was able to sort out those qualities in himself that truly constituted his more basic personality, thereby achieving a greater sense of personal autonomy. At the same time he learned how powerful the influence of relationships could be on his own feelings and behavior and how complex the forces that draw people together or pull them apart really are.

The relationships that the formerly married person establishes may set the ground work for another marriage. They may not. Asking yourself what you can do to zero in on a relationship that will bring you love and happiness and lead to marriage is a little like asking yourself what you can do to make a million dollars in the next three years. The real question is how can you establish a good life with what you have at hand and, at the same time, remain open to the unexpected.

SOME GUIDELINES FOR THOSE IN SEARCH OF NEW LOVE RELATIONSHIPS:

- Do keep an open mind about marrying again. Because it didn't work the first time is no reason to assume it won't the second.

- Explore a variety of new relationships. They offer chances to compare and contrast how you relate to different kinds of people, and you can learn a good deal about yourself in the process. These will also free you of any attachments that linger to a former husband or wife or way of life.

• Learn to live with uncertainty. No one can force the future. Coincidence plays too big a role.

• Accept the possibility that you may stay single and never marry again. If you can do this, you will be free to choose more wisely and from a greater number of options.

• Do not allow yourself to be so preoccupied with the need to find that "special relationship" in a hurry that you look at every new person in your life as a prospective husband or wife. Enjoy each involvement for its own sake.

• Don't assume that sex has to be offered lightly and be a part of each new relationship. If you believe personal closeness and sexual intimacy go hand and hand, live by your standard.

• True, it is a mistake to think that sex is irrelevant to a good marriage, but don't assume that an exciting sexual liaison is necessarily a love relationship.

• Do not let a misplaced sense of fidelity unwisely lock you into a relationship. Narrowing the field prematurely can be fatal.

• Above all, don't sell yourself short. Give yourself time to recover your wits and sense of self-esteem and give any relationship that you value the time and opportunity it needs to evolve.

There is no computer you can feed your name and credentials into that will come up with the right partner.

You can do all the obvious things—spend a week at the Club Med in Martinique and accept every invitation to a party that you receive and find a job where single men and women will be working with you or move from the suburbs back to the city where the action appears to be livelier—and still not meet someone you feel is right. Of course, if you do none of these things and, instead, isolate yourself and take no steps to reconstruct your social life, nothing at all can happen. You cannot live in a closet.

But assuming you have taken reasonable steps to meet people, it is crucial that you abandon the concept that you can find a road map that will lead you to romance and marriage. Coincidence plays too big a part in what happens to us all. People who are married a second time must admit that meeting and getting to know the person they married was usually the result of a chain of circumstances that they could not have predicted in advance and over which they had limited control.

If there is one rule to follow that cuts across the infinite variety of circumstances that newly single people find themselves in it is to acquire greater knowledge of themselves so that the relationships that they form can be sound and valid and to derive even more understanding of themselves through these relationships. There is no room for dishonesty here. To allow yourself to be taken advantage of, emotionally, sexually, financially, for the sake of having a relationship can only be done at great personal risk. To take advantage of someone who is struggling to rebuild a life—the divorce lawyer who seduces the client in his office in the name of restoring morale; the woman who, in spite of the sense of honesty that women's liberation demands, still looks on a man as a "catch"—is to add more confusion and hurt to the anguish such a person already knows only too well.

Self-knowledge is of more than moral importance. It is eminently practical. For the better you know yourself, the more likely you will be to pursue the kind of relationships that will not only serve you well but also be constructive for the person with whom you are involved. This search for insight is the only road to "liberation." Through it you can arrive at the point when you can make a really free decision as to whether to marry again or not. And you can shake free of motivations that might otherwise predispose you, should you marry again, to make another mistake.

5

Remarriage on the Rebound

One of the major challenges of the period that follows the end of a marriage is to genuinely extricate oneself from emotional entanglements that still survive. Only in this way is it possible to achieve sufficient freedom to make an intelligent choice whether to marry again or not and, if so, to whom. A 40 percent failure rate for second marriages is a rather high figure for men and women who, having been through a marriage before, might be expected to know better. A frequent failing that accounts for such a picture is the fact that the selection itself is poorly made. This, in turn, is often the result of motivations that are based on residual attachments to the former marriage.

The nature of the former marriage can influence the timing and choice of the second one. It is not unusual for people emerging battered from divorce to say they will swear off marriage for a long time or altogether, only to find themselves marrying again, in a short while, to someone whom they see primarily in reference to their former husband or wife—a person who is quite similar or one who represents the opposite extreme. Either situation can be a serious problem.

The limits are usually clearly set in the separation agreement when it comes to property. Visitation rights are spelled out. But no such agreement exists to deal with feelings. This is a responsibility left for the person himself to work out. And unless the reasons for a marriage's failure are quite apparent—repeated episodes of infidelity, alcoholism, dramatic evidence of incompatibility—you can find it very difficult to sort the pieces out and get a handle on what went wrong. Were you unsuited to each other from the beginning? Was there a series of stresses—parents dying, economic problems, problems with children—that tore you apart? Sexual dissatisfaction? Misunderstandings that never were resolved? Or did you feel you had just grown apart, or that one of you had grown at a faster rate than the other? Was life together suffocating? Often, however, the explanations that you come upon never seem quite enough to explain the disaster. You may be taken by surprise. As one man described, "I thought everything was fine until a few months before it all ended. I was stunned to find out that my wife had often thought of leaving me for most of the fourteen years of our marriage and that she had stuck it out as a matter of principle. I still don't understand it."

To counteract such bewilderment, many people construct webs of distorted memories and allow themselves to be guided by them. Weaknesses in the relationship or in the former husband or wife are exaggerated, concealing the strengths that may have existed as well. A couple may have shared a strong sense of parental responsibility and thoroughly enjoyed family life together, yet all that is recalled later is that they found themselves with little else in common and nothing to talk about once the children were grown. Another couple may have had many interests and viewpoints in common, sharing the bond of a strong emotional rapport and personal admiration, yet all they remember is that their sexual relationship was less than they were encouraged to think it should be.

When, after divorce, such problem areas are magnified, this skewed perception can constitute, to a dangerous degree, the basis of new relationships and the search for another partner. When Ronnie Morgan was nineteen and a freshman in college, she eloped. Martin was twenty-five. Ronnie was then still living with her family just outside San Diego and Martin was attached to the naval base there. They had met at a dance, seen each other a few times after that, and finally slept together—reluctantly on her part—one night in a motel. Conservatively brought up, she felt an immediate wave of guilt. She would lie awake at night, frightened, confused, trying to figure it all out, and always ending up with the conclusion that since this was her first complete sexual experience and in spite of the fact that it was not terribly pleasant, she would probably have to marry Martin. When she asked her mother what she should do—without, of course, mentioning all the details of the motel incident—her mother told her father, who exploded with a severe lecture about irresponsibility. She started to cry. He became angry and told her to go to her room until she could straighten out her thinking. That night she ran off with Martin.

They were married for three years, living in a garden apartment near the base. Although they were only a few miles away, she rarely saw her family. Occasionally her mother would meet her for lunch, but her father refused to talk to her at all. Ronnie worked as a secretary. She wanted a child but was afraid to have one, largely because she was unhappy. It did not take her long to realize she had made a mistake. Martin drank too much and at times would become viciously angry over nothing. He spent much of his free time watching baseball on television. She had little interest in baseball. They had very few friends.

When she was twenty-two she decided she had had enough. She left Martin a note one day, consulted a lawyer, and set in motion the steps necessary to get a divorce. At first, her husband pleaded with her to stay, but on finding out that she was not going to make any financial demands on him, he went along with it. Although her family was quite willing, at this point, for her to return home, she felt that she had to become independent. So she moved to San Francisco, where she found a good job and a nice apartment. She enrolled in night classes and started working again toward her bachelor's degree.

She was free, but it was only the most tenuous kind of freedom. At night she would sometimes have nightmares of Martin materializing in her apartment and forcing her to go back to him. Sometimes, in her loneliness, she found herself wishing suddenly that he would. As her thoughts began to crystallize, replacing vague anxieties and apprehension, she came to the conclusion that the relationship had not worked because her husband had been too immature, too dependent on her, uneducated, ill-mannered. All of her impressions were accurate. The error in her logic, however, was to look at these factors out of the context of her complete experience and to decide that she should only allow herself to become involved with a man who was the very opposite on all counts.

As a result she did not permit herself to form any meaningful relationships with men who were under thirty. They were too young. She was very sensitive to the slightest evidence of what she regarded as coarseness, even an occasional "damn" that might appear in the conversation. She set her sights on finding an older man, preferably someone who was involved in a profession and who would be quite independent. And so the detection system that operates to make men and women aware of one another's presence was, in her case, jammed, and she failed even to notice many men who might well have been suited to her.

After about a year she changed jobs and became a secretary in a large law firm. The man she worked for was a partner in his mid-forties. He had been divorced for eight years. The rumor she heard was that his former wife had had severe psychiatric problems and that he could no longer take the scenes and hospitals and shock treatments and all that went with it. He did have custody of his children. She liked that. He had an aura of competence and strength.

It was not hard for her to set things up. She made a point of being early on the job and working late. She bought herself a new wardrobe. When obvious measures failed to attract his attention, she tried a special tack—an intuitive application of Skinnerian conditioning principles—that finally worked. Whenever he was in the office, she made a point of being away from her desk. To find her, he had to look for her. It was a gamble but one that paid off. Instead of just getting angry and telling her to be more efficient or leave, her boss became intrigued by her now you see me, now you don't behavior. He asked her out to dinner.

They were married six months later. It took Ronnie only a few months to discover she had made another mistake. "No wonder his wife went out of her mind," she thought. It was an oversimplified but by no means entirely irrelevant conclusion. To begin with, he was frequently impotent. He was also intolerant of any show of emotion. Once, when she received some news from home about her mother's health, she began to cry. His reaction was to turn to her and say, dispassionately, "I don't like tears. I'll take a walk and maybe, by the time I get back, you'll have pulled yourself together." He did add something about being unhappy to hear the news about her mother.

Martin had been indolent. Her new husband was a workaholic. What she interpreted as a special kind of self-sufficiency was, in fact, the behavior of a man who had no choice but to work long hours, obsessed about details and afraid of making mistakes. At home he was a soft-spoken tyrant. He insisted that she stop working, so she did. He opposed her wish to continue her studies. It was not unusual for him to come home from work and survey the house, running his finger along the furniture and window sills, checking for traces of dust. If he found some, he said nothing. He would just look troubled.

Ronnie became increasingly despondent. Her unhappiness was compounded by her recognition of the fact that she had made the same mistake twice. Furthermore, to come to terms with this and resolve it meant that, to herself and to the world, she would be doubly a failure. She consulted a psychiatrist. When her husband discovered this, he was enraged, and when asked to visit the doctor himself, he flatly refused. Within a few months Ronnie went south to visit her family and never returned. She had very painfully discovered the hard way that it was a serious error in judgment to base one's selection of a new marriage primarily on what was lacking or problematic in a former one.

Such a situation can actually develop before one's first marriage ends in the form of an extramarital affair—the emotionally and sexually meaningful involvement that begins, by definition, while you are still married. The origins of many affairs can be found in the flaws that the marriage itself presents. If, for example, you cannot express certain resentments at home and get them sorted out—you may not even be aware that they are there—you may express your hostility toward your husband or wife by becoming involved with someone else. If you really want to cause pain or if you feel guilty, you may leave bits and pieces of evidence around so that you will eventually be discovered.

An affair can also begin because of insufficient love and support, fueled by poor self-regard that may originate from or be reinforced by a poor marital relationship. On the surface, at least, the affair is frequently fulfilling—psychologically, intellectually, sexually. It flourishes for a while because it is new, it is intense, it fills a specific need, and, most significantly, it is outside the mainstream of one's life.

One of the troubles with an affair is that as time passes, months and sometimes years, it is easy to forget where the mainstream of one's life really is. There is usually an attempt to relocate and rechannel it.

One may move to break off the affair, or one may feel impelled to end the marriage. Only under rare circumstances can the affair last indefinitely. It is time-consuming. It often requires a great deal of skill at deception. Usually one or the other person involved presses to turn it into a marriage.

If, in fact, you have found something in the affair that was missing in your marriage, the end of the affair may leave you with the painful realization that what had been missing all along is a feature of human relatedness that can never be developed within your own marriage because the material from which to create it is just not there. The popular myth that an affair can improve one's marriage is closer to fiction than fact. No one can be all things to anybody. Very few people are able to accept, with resignation, that what they have discovered in the affair—a new level of understanding, passion, sharing—is sufficient unto itself and that they may have to spend the rest of their lives living with a memory of it. It is also difficult to settle for the fact that whatever enrichment they may have found in the affair does not require the affair itself to go on for any positive results to endure. There is an old adage in research that is often forgotten even by scientists and that could well apply to many affairs: What is not there can still act. But most of us are not convinced of this at all.

The pressure to resolve the frustration of an affair is often intense. You may find it hard to imagine life without the other person. Or, if your marriage ends—triggered perhaps by the scent of perfume on your suit or frequent absences in the afternoon when you should have been attending to children coming home from school—you may suddenly find yourself confronted with the need to consider seriously and for the first time whether you want this relationship, once peripheral, to become the central focus for your life. The situation is not unlike that of the person who, having always been able to make enormous profits in the stock market as long as it was a game, finds that when he finally does have some cash to buy stocks, his judgment suddenly seems to become much more fallible.

Practical questions suddenly begin to pass through one's mind. It was easy to overlook her habit of lateness when you weren't living together; what would it be like to have this as a daily routine? His aversion to social activities was fine when the two of you spent all your time together, but what would this do to your life if you were married? How will your family accept this new person, especially your children? Will your former partner find out that the two of you had been involved before you were divorced and become particularly vindictive? Is the age difference too great? What about having more children? Do you really have enough in common to make a go of it? Is there enough respect? Can either of you be trusted not to have another affair once you are married to each other?

Some relationships and marriages that stem from affairs can and do work well. But, by and large, they can be risky, since they are so often based on motivations that stem from problems operating in the former marriage. They may represent a haven from general unhappiness. They may offer the one quality that the marriage lacked. Once pushed into reality, however, and tested in the daylight, they commonly present a whole new set of problems that can be as difficult to solve as those left behind.

Unresolved feelings about a former marriage or partner can influence your judgment adversely in other ways too. Marrying on the rebound is a good example. Loneliness and the feeling of being rejected, even when you have been the instigator of the divorce, can propel you blindly into another marriage.

Revenge can serve the same purpose. So can pride. When one partner remarries, the other may be tempted, as a matter of pride, to follow suit.

Moreover, the personality of a former husband or wife does not have to be the primary point of reference. You may be anxious to marry again to reestablish a way of life that has been lost—or to reject one that, at the moment, seems obsolete and detrimental. Drew Ordway and his wife had built up a very successful life together. They had a ten-room house in Locust Valley, New York, on Long Island's North Shore. In the summers they traveled through Europe. Drew was an advertising executive. He and his wife were active in various community groups. Their three children attended private schools. The rest of their lives stretched out in front of them predictably, solidly, or so it seemed.

Shortly after his forty-fifth birthday Drew was faced with a series of personal crises. His business had another poor year, the second one in a row, and he began to question his judgment. He was also faced with putting his elderly, senile father in a nursing home. Moreover, two of their teenage youngsters were doing quite poorly in school, and one, a sixteen-year-old daughter, became pregnant and had an abortion. Drew and his wife, Margaret, began to blame each other for their children's problems. Drew was depressed but totally unaware of it and so arrived at what he thought was a logical course of action: He became convinced that his entire life-style was at fault and suggested that they live apart for a while.

"I've had all I ever want of that kind of life," he swore to himself. He found a comfortable two-bedroom apartment in a new building on Third Avenue in Manhattan. He let his hair grow and began dressing in slacks, sports shirt and jacket. He spent his free time in coffeeshops and singles places. In the summer he shared a house with a dozen other unmarried men and women. Dating only girls in their mid-twenties, he went out of his way to choose those whom he thought of—when he allowed himself to admit it—as "hippie" types, girls with long brown hair who were dabbling with graduate studies in art appreciation or working in little boutiques in Greenwich Village and who, above all, were without any trace of the kind of social or economic background that he was shedding.

"Okay, so it's adolescent," he told one friend, "but I

never really had an adolescence." Convinced that he never wanted to return to the kind of life he had always known and not wanting to break up his romantic relationship (his sixth such) with Denice, he asked her to marry him. Denice was twenty-three. She worked as a waitress in the day and went to school at night, studying modern dance. With considerable reluctance ("I don't want to be hemmed in by commitments") she accepted his proposal. Their marriage had lasted three months when, one afternoon, he came home unexpectedly to find her in bed with the superintendent's son. "What's wrong?" she asked.

If you are being influenced by attachments to your first marriage, such an influence can as easily be a positive as a negative one. Originally, after all, there were rather significant forces that drew the couple together. With few exceptions there are happy memories as well as tragic ones. The lingering desire to be back with that particular person can be quite strong at times, so strong, in fact, that many men and women may be lulled into looking for someone else to marry by the wish to find the same kind of person—without, of course, that particular problem that ruined the marriage. Physical appearance may well be similar, with a second husband or wife bearing a close resemblance to a former one. This is often no coincidence. Moreover, there may often be a personality resemblance as well.

As time passes, and especially if there are no vivid reminders of trouble—angry phone calls, bitter letters, subpoenas and the like—you may actually start thinking that things were not really that bad after all. Sometimes they were not, and as the pain wears off, a better perspective takes over. The second marriage may even end up being to the very same person one was formerly married to.

Often, however, the past becomes idealized. You forget

how bad things were. You want to go home, and if you can't, you want to come as close as possible to finding a similar situation. As one man put it, "I really liked the way my wife handled people. She was a great hostess and a really good cook. I liked our friends. I liked the sound of her voice. I liked making love to her. What I really want is *her* again, but without the selfish streak that she had that nearly drove me crazy. When I walk down the street and look at women, it's her type that turns me on. In fact, I can't even get interested in other women unless they remind me of her."

As long as you are still too attached to a former husband or wife—whether still attracted to them, looking for complete opposites, trying to locate someone without the one trait that upset you, or governed by an "I'll show them" attitude—it is wiser to refrain from making any commitment to a new marriage. If you still send her flowers on her birthday (which she does not thank you for and does not want) and if you still follow what is happening to him in his career or keep track of the women he takes out (keeping up to date through acquaintances), be careful not to assume that you are ready for another try at marriage.

If you spend much of your energy trying to think up new ways to avoid paying child support or fresh tactics to legally harass him, or if you delight in running into her in a restaurant with a pretty young girl on your arm, or if you are especially pleased to know that your social life is going ahead full steam while his is a shambles, watch out. The chances are that you have not yet freed yourself enough from the past to make a new marriage work.

There is, of course, no graduation day. The bond that was never entirely disappears. Events occur gradually. Before and after intermesh indistinguishably. There is never a point at which we can feel so completely detached that we allow ourselves, diploma in hand, to proceed into a new marriage smugly.

If you wonder whether or not you are free enough from the influences of your past life or former partner to make an intelligent and independent decision to remarry, ask yourself the following questions. The more affirmative answers you give, the more you should reconsider your motives for remarriage at this time.

- Does the person you are thinking of marrying strongly resemble your former husband or wife in appearance?

- Is the personality characteristic you most value in the person you love the very one your former spouse seemed to lack?

- Is the same source of conflict that caused you so much trouble in your former marriage—competitiveness or jealousy, for instance—present in this relationship too, perhaps showing up in a different way?

- Do you find that you cannot really be yourself in this relationship without encountering the same conflicts that arose in your first marriage?

- Is the battle that characterized your former marriage and that was associated with its failure still going on, with your full cooperation?

- Did your present relationship begin as an affair while you were still married?

- Do you find yourself categorically rebelling against anything that reminds you of your former spouse or of your way of life together?

- Are you still preoccupied with what happens to your ex-wife or husband, to the extent of feeling jealous or envious when good things happen to her or him and pleased when you hear bad news?

- Are you looking for someone who is just like your former spouse except, of course, without that one trait that caused all the trouble?

- Do you miss what you have lost?

Working out the insights about your past marriage and testing yourself in new relationships go hand in hand to make you truly free of the past. Comparison and contrast both help to restore vision. You may not know what it is to have a mutually satisfying kind of closeness with a man or woman who is capable of it until after you have emerged, scarred to be sure, from a marriage to someone who was demanding and ungiving from the start. You may not know what sexual fulfillment can be like until you find it with someone else after years of being married to someone whose interest in sex was feigned or lacking in sensitivity. You may not have learned until in the setting of a new relationship that people who care about each other can fight and argue and clear the air and reconciliate, coming together again with more closeness than before; all you may have known previously was an angry impasse that went on for weeks, without any making up; or disagreements that never found their way to the light of day, festering, out of sight, for years.

Postponing the decision to marry again is generally the best policy. It permits time for insight into a former marriage to crystallize. It also provides the opportunity to experiment with new relationships. There is no rule with regard to how long such a transition takes. For some people it may take years; for others, it may not.

In any case, by following such advice, you will be less

likely to be goaded by unresolved feelings into unwanted and complicated relationships. Things can settle down. You can allow yourself to change. Most important, you can begin to question the basis of your previous marriage, the problems you encountered in it, and the pattern of your new involvements from another very important angle: Is there something within you, you should ask yourself, that influenced you to choose someone to marry with whom unhappiness was inevitable?

6

Unconscious Blueprints

Children growing up imitate the attitudes and behavior of their parents. They speak like them. They walk like them. They think like them. One of the tasks of adolescence is to shake off some of these assumptions and patterns in order to develop a stronger sense of one's self and become freer to determine one's future.

This process is never complete and, all too often, quite inadequate. Significant traces of an upbringing reside within the marrow of our personalities, for better or worse. They are largely unconscious and so exert their influence on how we experience what we experience in an unseen though powerful manner. One such imprint contains our earliest impressions of what the relationship between a man and a woman is like and what marriage itself is all about.

If, for instance, the equilibrium between your parents was such that one or another parent was extraordinarily dominant—the strong mother, weaker father syndrome or its reverse—this model of family life has been indelibly etched into your unconscious. Its strength derives in no small measure from the fact that, at the time that you first perceived it, you had nothing else with which to compare this impression.

It is common, in adolescence, to go through a phase in which one rejects the parental values and way of life to some degree, regardless of their character. When young people, adolescents or older, state adamantly that they do not want the kind of marriage that their parents had, they may be distorting a perfectly good relationship into an unfulfilling one. Or their rebellion against the model may be rooted in good cause. There may not have been much affection between their parents. Communication may have been poor. The household atmosphere may have been charged with conflict. Love and respect between the two may have died a long time ago.

It is quite apparent that one of the reasons why marriage has fallen into such disrepute over the last few years is the fact that many young people take a good hard look at what their parents' marriages were like and, correctly or not, come away disillusioned in the very concept of marriage. Many of them, however, are actually in touch with the very real risk that they run of making a similarly unsatisfactory commitment, even if this awareness is intuitive rather than consciously thought through.

In order to understand the nature of this risk, we must have a clear picture of how the unconscious works. It is an active force that influences how we perceive ourselves, how we view reality, and that enters into our day-to-day behavior and the important choices that we make in life. The less we are aware of its character, the more influential it can be, and the force of the unconscious is particularly strong when one has not successfully gone through the stages of separation from family and the establishment of one's own personality that are necessary to the adequate completion of adolescence.

However disguised it may be behind an ostensibly rational approach, a strong urge exists in most people that propels them to seek out the same kind of marriage that their parents had or to go to the opposite extreme and literally reverse the pattern. It is in the nature of the unconscious that its drives are absolute, expressed in black and white terms, without shades of gray. The daughter of a capricious, tyrannical, problematic father is likely to seek out a man who is indecisive, excessively dependent on her, quiet and accommodating, to blot out the original blueprint. She then may find herself married to a man whom she does not fundamentally respect and with whom she must live in the kind of equilibrium that does not suit her. A young man who comes from a home in which his mother made most of the important decisions and gave little attention to the opinions of a somewhat reticent father has a good chance of marrying a woman who, no matter how pleasant and compatible she may seem during their courtship, gradually emerges over time as the independent and controlling partner; not uncommonly she herself may come from a home in which the mother was the stronger force.

So it can work either way—movement toward a marriage that resembles that of one's parents or a marriage that is sought out in a desperate attempt to avoid the original model. Whatever conscious motivations may sway people in choosing their marriages, the role of the unconscious in their behavior is often formidable. People who make the same mistake twice, or even more often, are usually still under the influence of an unconscious theme. They seem to have a sixth sense for choosing partners with problems that confirm their worst fears about marriage. "I must have a thing for dependent women," one thirty-eight-year-old salesman recounted, looking back on two marital failures. "Either that or I bring it out in them." His first wife was a pleasant, quiet woman—unsure of herself but in such a way that she appealed to him. He liked the idea of taking care of her. "But I didn't know what I was in for. She'd call me at work and ask how long to cook dinner, as if I knew. She never could think of any plans for things we could do together. She was constantly asking me for reassurance about her looks. She had very few friends. It was like living in a prison."

The second time he married he chose a woman who seemed very outgoing and independent. But a few months after they were married, she began to do less and less on her own. First, she refused to drive a car even though she had done so for many years, claiming that she was now afraid to have an accident. Then she developed a fear of flying so that, whenever he had to travel any distance, he was forced to go alone. Slowly but surely—as she felt anxious about going to parties or having people to their home for dinner—their social life contracted and finally evaporated. "There I was, living in a box again."

The common denominator in his two marriages was the helpless behavior manifested by each of his wives—the first, flagrantly; the second, concealed behind phobic fears. He had deliberately sought it out the first time, but in spite of his conscious efforts, something within him intuitively sensed the dependency the second time and found its influence no less compelling.

The catalyst in his poor selection was his mother's personality. She had been a withdrawn and unspontaneous woman, given to moodiness and lacking in self-confidence. "I remember, as a young man, seeing myself as a gallant rescuer. I loved the old Errol Flynn films, watching him swashbuckle his way to save Olivia de Havilland. I can see my marriages now as having turned out to be a kind of grotesque parody of them, with my wives' lack of independence luring me on and then suffocating me."

Not surprisingly, in the selection of marital partners, many people choose someone who can play a reciprocal role to their own unconscious model while fitting into the other person's hidden blueprints as well. Thus an equilibrium can be established that enables a marriage to endure for some time, often permanently. The man from a home in which his mother was a woman given to incessant criticism marries a woman whose own mother behaved in essentially a similar way. As the marriage progresses, he becomes more and more like her father in his attitudes as she grows to resemble his mother. Unhappy though they may be, the surface incompatibility is frequently balanced against the deeper congruence that forms a powerful bond between them.

In its most severe form, this kind of linkage can become what psychiatrists have called *folie-à-deux,* the craziness of two. This is a condition in which two people become so intensely interwoven with each other on an unconscious level that one of the partners can literally go mad in response to the demands of the script dictated by the other. For instance, if a man's mother had been a severe alcoholic and he marries a woman who is both appropriately suggestible and comes from a background in which alcoholism played a significant role, she may herself develop a serious drinking problem in response to his unconscious expectations and in spite of his overt disapproval. People who share such a *folie-à-deux* are usually very reluctant to break it up, in spite of the fact that the well-being of each, if not the sanity, usually depends on ending the relationship.

Harold Ward's parents had had a good marriage, not perfect to be sure, but they had loved each other, been demonstrative in their affection for one another, and created a warm and open family life.

Harold's father worked in a factory. His mother did part-time work as a bookkeeper. His brothers and sisters never went beyond high school. But Harold, the star of the family, having won a scholarship to college, having gone on to study engineering, and feeling well on the way to more success, was determined to marry a girl who was more educated than his family, more social, and who would anchor him more securely in his new world.

From the first year of his marriage on, he began to experience paralyzing episodes of depression. These would last for four months or so, during which time he found it impossible to work effectively. He occasionally found the thought of suicide drifting through his mind but was usually able to fight it off quickly. Despite the fact that he had never experienced moods like these before, it never occurred to Harold that his marriage might be a major factor until, during a particularly intense bout of depression, he sought psychiatric help. By then he had been married for ten years and had three children. "My wife disapproved of my going to the doctor and, when he asked to see her, refused to cooperate. As I began to see how our relationship was causing my moods, I couldn't believe it at first. It seemed farfetched, too complicated, but now that we've been divorced for a couple of years and I haven't had any more episodes, I am utterly convinced of it."

Harold's wife had come from a well-to-do family, had attended an Ivy League women's college and was one of the most intelligent women he had ever met. What he ignored was the significance of other aspects of her family background—"a horror scene," in Harold's words, which she had glamorized to him and to herself and into which she had no insight. Her father had suffered with severe depressions and had committed suicide when she was eight years old. Her mother had married again, briefly, four years later, to a reformed alcoholic who began to drink heavily again a few months after their wedding. Bitter and vindictive, her mother had instilled in her and her sisters a deep hatred toward and distrust of men. Harold had met his wife at a time in her life when she was struggling to shake off her mother's influence and denying to herself any similar resentments by being particularly loving and submissively considerate with the men she dated.

Throughout their marriage she remained superficially congenial. She did everything that one would expect of a good wife. She kept a neat and meticulous home, was a good hostess and a responsible parent. Even though she was sexually frigid, she was always willing to sleep with Harold and often feigned orgasm. Her unconscious images, however, were unchanged. A husband and father were seen as either a man subject to dangerous depressions or a potential alcoholic. In either case, he was someone to be neither trusted nor counted on and would probably, in the final analysis, desert her and the children. Her unconscious hostility was communicated subliminally. When their marriage ended, she was convinced that Harold was the sole cause of their unhappiness and her deep expectations were confirmed.

The themes that are contained in the unconscious and that relate to marriage may show up, to some degree, in the relationships that you established prior to marriage. The kind of women that you prefer and the sort of man who turns you on will be selected, in part, by these images. But one of the reasons why living together before marriage, in and of itself, is no solution to this problem rests in the fact that the unconscious models are somehow activated by the formalization of the marriage itself. Moreover, they are again reinforced as children are born and the couple become parents. These events put the individual into closer contact with the threads that connect him to his original family.

Moreover, even when you are relatively free of such motivations at the time you decide to marry, they can come into play afterward to shape the relationship in such a way as to conform to the model. A little-known fact is that women as well as men tend to project onto the person they marry expectations and conflicts that stem from their earlier relationship with their mothers. This is not surprising, since the mother constitutes for most of us our earliest impressions of the world outside ourselves. A woman whose mother was stern and ungiving may develop a strong need for repeated demonstrations of affection from her husband. However much he may care for her, she feels he never shows enough love and attention. She then may seek it again and again from him, insistently, aggressively, only making him feel inadequate, angry, frustrated, and driving him further and further away. A man whose relationship with an oversolicitous mother may have set the stage for considerable dependency on women but at the same time made him basically very hostile toward them may find it impossible to deal honestly and directly with his wife. Instead, as some do, he may turn to extramarital affairs to hurt her for not loving him enough—something beyond any woman's ability—and at the same time build a bridge to escape from his marriage. On the surface, he may appear to other women to be a glamorous, gallant, highly masculine figure, but underneath he is actually caught in a vicious, destructive cycle of reenacting with any woman he is deeply involved with scripts that originated in the earliest years of his life.

It must be apparent by now that the better the marriage of our parents has been, the better our own chances of making a good marriage. This is no guarantee, of course. Circumstances can intervene, as they did in the case of Harold Ward, who was embroiled in a *folie-à-deux,* to distract us from healthy and constructive inner messages. Nor does it mean that if our parent's marriages were poor, or ended themselves in divorce, that we are doomed to follow suit. There are too many instances of adversity promoting very positive ends. The very determination to make a marriage work, for example, that allows a couple to survive and learn from the storms that usually accompany marriage may have been born of a strong need not to repeat parents' mistakes.

Nonetheless, as complex as it may seem to the uninitiated, the success of any marriage depends heavily on the amount of insight that one can gain into the influence of these early blueprints and the amount of freedom that one can achieve from that influence. Rarely does a marriage end in divorce without unconscious components having contributed to the problems in the relationship and often the selection of divorce as a solution to those problems.

Here again is a cogent argument for taking the time and making the effort necessary to gain as much insight into yourself as you can before moving into another marriage. The autonomy as a person that you seek involves not only an understanding of yourself as you are now but also a rather vivid and graphic picture of the family that you grew up in and how their influence may have not only shaped your character but actually become part of your own set of values and attitudes. It is really not hard to sit down for a few moments, from time to time, and ask yourself such questions as "What was the nature of my parents' relationship?" "How well did they communicate?" "What kind of sexual life do I think they had?" "How did my former marriage resemble or differ from theirs?"

The answers will not all come at once. You will, as we all do, tend to alter the past in your memories, remembering some, forgetting some, exaggerating some, overemphasizing some. But over a period of time you will be able to see the design more clearly. Your first marriage itself may offer important clues. When you ask, "What went wrong?" consider the possibility that some of the areas of conflict and incompatibility might bear a strong stamp of resemblance to your former partner's original family or your own. Certain characteristics, to which you may have been extremely sensitive, may have been less problematic in themselves but primarily provocative because of your own vulnerability to them, a vulnerability that stemmed from your earlier experiences in life.

While it is indeed an oversimplification, you can usually select several specific criteria to use to evaluate the influence of your family's structure and mode of operation on your own image of marriage. There is a great deal to be learned by contrasting your former spouse's family pattern and that of the person you are now planning to marry, as well as your own. To define the characteristics of each family, you should consider:

1. Who was more powerful, father or mother?
2. How much communication existed between the parents and within the family?
3. How much demonstrable affection was there between parents? What do you know about their sexual relationship?
4. Was there a cooperative pulling together in most endeavors, or did each member pull against the others?

5. How much psychological insightfulness and flexibility was there?
6. Was there a good deal of selfishness or a spirit of generosity?
7. What were the attitudes toward achievement and approaches to child rearing?
8. What was the religious and socioeconomic status?
9. What were the most important family values?
10. Were there special trouble spots, such as divorce, mental illness or unusual cruelty, or alcoholism?

To this list you should add the quality of your own relationship with each of your parents and do the same for your former mate and partner to be.

Make out a chart for yourself, such as the one that follows, using a simple plus or minus rating system to indicate whether a particular quality was clearly present or absent. If you don't know the answer, put a question mark. If that quality may have been there in part but was not really well defined, put both a plus and a minus. This approach is not definitive, but it can be quite revealing.

The fact that there is a high degree of correspondence between the portrait of your own family interaction and that of your wife's does not, by any means, indicate that your marriage is a good one. It does mean that you are, on an unconscious level, compatible. But what is important is whether this compatibility lies in strengths or weaknesses. The fact that there are areas of difference, by the same token, does not mean that your marriage is doomed. But it does mean that some basic adjustments may have to be made.

Consider the case of a forty-year-old teacher whose answers are shown on the sample chart. This man had to watch his tendency to be too dominant in his second

Significant characteristics	Husband's parents' marriage	First wife's parents' marriage	Second wife's parents' marriage
Dominant father	+	−	−
Dominant mother	−	+	−
Good communications	+	−	+
Affectionate	+	−	+
Sexual adjustment	?	−	?
Cooperativeness	+	−	+
Thwarting, bickering	+	+	−
Insight and flexibility	+	−	+
Generosity	+	−	+
Valued achievement	+	−	+
Permissiveness	−	+	−
Socioeconomic similarity		no	yes
Religious similarity		yes	yes
Divorce	−	+	−
Alcoholism	−	+	−
Good relationship to own father	+	−	+
Good relationship to own mother	+	+	+

Number of corresponding parental qualities between husband and former wife—3; between husband and second wife—14.

marriage to a woman whose parents had had a more equitable balance of power. He also had to resist a tendency to bicker and thwart, learning how to give more of himself emotionally to the new marriage. In his former marriage, however, it is easy to identify the gross differences in unconscious expectations and attitudes. The marriage lasted for nearly twelve years, largely because of his skill at adaptation and acquiesence to his wife's quite different model of marital relationships. It ended explosively when he could no longer maintain his compliance.

A former marriage, for some people, serves as a training ground. During it, a psychological contract with the past may have been completed and one may now be permitted to proceed toward building a new kind of marriage free of such emotional entanglements. Most of the time, however, it is far better to search for common denominators running through a series of relationships that you establish after you are single again that will reveal the nature of your hidden preferences. It is far wiser to work this out while still single than through another marriage embarked upon in unforgivable innocence.

7

Marrying Again

You are finally thinking of marrying again. You're nervous and you don't have the old confidence you had the first time, for, no matter how right you think it is, you are acutely aware of the risk that accompanies your determination to make it work. And sometimes you wonder what your real motivations are.

The decision to remarry is too complex a choice to be attributed to any single motivation. There are many. The desire to be married and a couple again in a couple's world and the economic and social benefits of marriage cross your mind. For many women marriage means companionship and for many men, the feeling of being settled in again, the end of empty refrigerators and empty rooms. It also means the right to file a joint income-tax return. If you had no children in your previous marriage, the wish to have a family can be an important spur. There is usually, of course, the desire to have someone special to share life with.

But when you stop to ask yourself, why now, why this particular person, all the reasons added up together may fail to convey the deeper and more powerful intent which often remains obscure or, in fact, may sometimes be frankly incomprehensible. As one man who had successfully remarried recalled: "I can't really say why I decided to marry again at that particular time. I was dating my present wife and I couldn't make up my mind whether to marry her or not. Then, one night, I was standing on the terrace of my apartment at about midnight when, suddenly, the whole sky lit up. It was during the Bay of Pigs invasion. I was terrified. It's got to be the end of the world, I thought. An atomic attack. And right after that I felt this tremendous urge telling me that if I lived through this I'd better marry this girl and get my life in order once and for all. Within a few minutes I realized that what I had seen was the explosion of propane tanks in the building under construction several miles away. Still, I went right to the phone and called her and asked her to marry me and she said yes."

If you wait a few years after a former marriage has ended before marrying again you will usually improve your chances of choosing well. You will have had that much more time to learn about yourself and understand your relationships with others, and you will be more likely to be governed by common sense than by wishful thinking and to have observed some of the following critical guidelines.

DON'T BELIEVE THE WORDS FROM THE MUSICAL *Guys and Dolls* THAT TELL YOU TO "MARRY THE MAN TODAY AND CHANGE HIS WAYS TOMORROW." MARRIAGE RARELY, IF EVER, MAKES A POOR RELATIONSHIP BETTER. Don't find yourself making the same mistake that one man did by violating this principle twice. At twenty-four he had married a woman whom he found boring and whose educational level was considerably below his own. She was extremely attractive, however, and he was convinced that his own wit and imagination would stimulate what he thought might be her potential. After a couple of years of married life, she had not changed at all, and he was sneaking around seeing other women, a pattern that continued until his divorce, two children and ten years later. The second time he married a bright, amusing women who enjoyed staying up until all hours of the night and, in contrast to his first wife, wanted a life full of fun. However, there was one problem. She drank much too much and too often. Again he was sure he could persuade her to change. By the end of the three years that their marriage lasted, she had been hospitalized several times to recover from severe bouts of drinking and he had acquired several scars to attest to her violent temper.

Be sure your interest and love are truly reciprocated. If you find yourself involved in a one-sided relationship, caring for someone far more than that person cares for you, your chances of making your marriage work are slim. You might succeed, through charm or subtle manipulation, in getting that person to marry you, but the odds are that neither time nor living together can bring your partner to feel feelings that were not there to begin with, except perhaps some guilt, depression, or outright defiance. You may find yourself pleading for signs of affection and unable to accept the fact that, though you married with passion, your new partner married for some other, less intense motive. The stakes are high. Honesty is essential. Romantic feelings and sexual excitement are important to the success of many second marriages, but they are only valid when they are shared.

Know the person you intend to marry as well as you can. What is it about this person that attracts you so? What potential do you see in him or her that you realistically feel you can nurture? Knowing someone not only includes impressions based strictly on your own contact with that person. You should find out a good deal about his or her past as well. If the man you are thinking of marrying was very promiscuous as a young bachelor, repeatedly unfaithful to his former wife and very free-wheeling after his divorce, you'd best ask yourself: What can I bring to this relationship that will be unique enough to guarantee his fidelity? If the woman you plan to marry has always been extravagant and your resources are decidedly limited, or if she complained her way in and out of her first marriage and she now hangs on your arm as if you were the answer to her prayers, be careful. People can and do change for the better, but not without considerable anguish, and it is best to witness a long period of improvement so that you can be reasonably sure it will last.

HAVE A CLEAR IDEA OF WHAT WENT WRONG IN YOUR OWN FORMER MARRIAGE AND PIECE TOGETHER A SOUND PICTURE OF YOUR POTENTIAL PARTNER'S FORMER MARRIAGE AS WELL. In doing so, be careful not to be too simplistic in your thinking. There are rarely only good guys and bad guys. It is to be hoped that by now you realize what your contributions to your first marriage's failure were and how you can minimize these in another and that the person you are considering for marriage has also abandoned the self-righteousness that so often goes along with divorce and can share with you a more intelligent and objective vision of his or her previous involvement.

LISTEN TO YOUR INTUITION. When you are on the verge of marrying again, you will experience some strong hunches. These may be positive: Moving toward marriage feels comfortable, the right way to go. Or they may be distressing; if so, they may seem at times to offend a rational appraisal, but only because you are unconsciously picking up information your conscious mind is blocking out. Though it could be only the normal anxiety everyone feels approaching a major life shift, it could be instead an important warning signal. A thirty-five-year-old woman described her intuitive experience as follows: "We had already made our wedding plans. We had told most of our friends. But I kept putting off telling either my parents or my children. Sometimes I'd reach for the phone to call my mother and my hand would literally freeze. I'd sit down with my children to talk with them about it, and I couldn't get the words out and I'd change the subject before mentioning it. My communication with my family had always been excellent, so I knew that if I had so much trouble there had to be something wrong, though I couldn't figure out what. So I put the marriage off. He was furious. We broke up. A year or so later I found out from a friend who also knew his former wife that he had some pretty peculiar sexual aberrations, like wanting to have pain inflicted on him, that would have horrified me. None of this had surfaced in our relationship, but I'm sure it would have, given time."

EVALUATE YOUR PROSPECTIVE MARRIAGE IN THE CONTEXT OF EVERYDAY LIFE. People behave differently under different circumstances, and it is important to see how well your relationship holds up under the ordinary stresses and challenges you will face as a couple. One of the disadvantages of marrying someone with whom you have been having an extramarital affair is that, for obvious reasons, it has not been grounded in day-to-day reality and hence has not been properly tested. Moreover, exposure to friends and family members whose judgment you trust and respect can give you valuable insights into the person you are thinking of marrying as well as into the quality of your relationship. While by no means infallible, a favorable consensus can be reassuring, and an unfavorable one should make you think twice. While your decision to remarry must, in the end, be your own and not unduly influenced by others, there is one opinion poll you cannot ignore—the attitude of your children and the nature of their relationship with your prospective husband or wife.

Expect to be upset as you move toward a second marriage, however convinced you may be that you are acting wisely. Another major change is about to take place in your life. A major shift is imminent in the world you have built as a single person. Everyone around you will be affected too, and what they say and how they behave will reveal this. Your children may ask whether, once you are married again, they will still visit you. You may go out to dinner with your future in-laws, just after they have learned you are going to marry their son. Hoping to please them, you tell them how much you love him. His mother, having had one vodka martini too many, interjects: "That's nice. Of course, my son could have had anyone he wanted." And his father soberly remarks: "You do know how much he's paying in alimony and child support, I suppose."

When you go to get the license, you must bring proof of your divorce, the document signed by the judge in Juarez. You may try to arrange to be married in your own church by your minister, only to discover that there are certain regulations about divorced people being married there. He directs you to another church down the street. Or you settle for a Justice of the Peace or a friend who is a judge or a nondenominational chapel like the one at the United Nations.

If you have both been married before, there will probably be no long white dresses and no tails. Only a few close friends and family and, of course, the children will attend. At the wedding you will be unable to keep from remembering the first time. It was the best party you had ever been to. Your family had decided that this would be the occasion to pay off all their accumulated social obligations. Over two hundred people came to the ceremony and the reception at the country club, and they all drank imported French champagne and ate beef Stroganoff. The orchestra played "I Love You Truly" and the Beatles were in vogue then, so no party could be complete without "I Want to Hold Your Hand" and "Yesterday." The bridesmaids were unmarried, and you hoped some of them might pair off with some of the ushers, most of whom were also single.

This time there is still champagne, but it is from upstate New York. The people are cheerful and laughing because, basically, people like a good wedding. It seems strange to have your children there; they act a lot quieter than they usually do. You have tried to make it easier for them by including them as bridesmaids or flower girls; in fact, one of your sons might even be asked to be the best man.

You want a simple wedding. It seems more genuine this way. But in the distant recesses of your mind you can hear the orchestra playing "Yesterday" and you recall your parents dancing together. You shake free of the memory by thinking that you didn't like beef Stroganoff anyway and wondering whatever happened to all those people who had come there, most of whom you haven't seen since.

As you wave goodbye, smiling, you suddenly feel a bit anxious and strangely sad, knowing that your second life as a single person is over. The loss runs deep. You have grown used to being on your own. The more successfully you have built a life for yourself, the more you may have come to enjoy the self-sufficiency it afforded. In ways too numerous to count, you have learned to be an individual. Now that too must be relinquished, somewhat, in order to meet one of the inherent demands of any remarriage, the creation of a new "we."

8

Creating a New "We"

Carolyn Chambers was cleaning out some old boxes she had stored inside the hall closet three years earlier when she first bought the house in Cape Cod. It was a sort of symbolic spring cleaning in preparation for her new life married to Ken Burton. Now forty-five, she had met Ken a year before, just after his wife had been killed in a car accident in California. He was the minister of the Episcopal church she attended. Now that they were married, they were going to be living together in the vicarage. Carolyn rather liked the idea of being a minister's wife.

She found, among all the clutter, an overstuffed brown envelope that released a mass of papers and old greeting cards. She paused over a card. She had designed it herself and had it printed when she was married before and living in Kansas City, a line drawing of a Christmas Tree and inside, neatly printed, "best wishes for a lovely holiday, Carolyn and Tim." The past reached out and pulled a nerve as she recalled how strongly she had felt identified with Carolyn and Tim. They had been building lives together. They had been raising a family together.

She had taken marriage very seriously and had delighted for a long time in the "we" of it.

Now there was to be another "we." And she felt a mixture of uncertainty and unreality, that "I've been here before" feeling. She was very much in love with Ken. She admired and respected him. She was convinced that their marriage would work. But during the three years that she had been very much on her own, working, raising her children, making new friends, Carolyn had developed a strong sense of her own abilities, which combined with the natural reticence someone who has emerged from one marriage feels about placing too much confidence and hope in a new one.

Her husband, Ken, had worn a wedding ring throughout his former marriage. This time he chose not to. Carolyn was sensitive to this, interpreting it at first as a sign of his reluctance to make a genuine commitment. It took her some time to realize that his gesture did not imply this at all but rather reflected his wish to make their marriage a fresh and different relationship with its own special character.

Ken too had trouble with settling into a new identity. For months, when he introduced Carolyn to new people, he would stumble over the word "wife" and had to consciously avoid using pet phrases that he had used toward his former wife. These would slip out every now and then, and Carolyn, depending on her mood at the time, would wince or be amused.

A sense of union can be delayed by frequent and unintentional reminders of the past. The yearly holiday card now addressed to a couple that no longer exists, the phone calls from people who may not realize that you're divorced, much less remarried, and letters from school administrators who assume that you are the parent of your partner's children conspire to make you feel that you have no business being where you are or that you have somehow stepped into someone else's shoes.

Daphne du Maurier described this confusion in a classic scene from *Rebecca:* "I took one [note paper] out and looked at it. . . . 'Mrs. M. de Winter' it said, and in the corner 'Manderley.' I put it back in the box again, and shut the drawer, feeling guilty suddenly, and deceitful, as though I were staying in somebody else's house and my hostess had said to me, 'Yes, of course, write letters at my desk,' and I had unforgivably, in a stealthy manner, peeked at her correspondence. . . .

"And when the telephone rang, suddenly, alarmingly, on the desk in front of me, my heart leapt and I started up in terror, thinking I had been discovered. I took the receiver off with trembling hands, and 'Who is it?' I said, 'who do you want?'. . . . 'Mrs. de Winter?' it said, 'Mrs. de Winter?'

" 'I'm afraid you have made a mistake,' I said. 'Mrs. de Winter has been dead for over a year.' I sat there, waiting, staring stupidly into the mouthpiece, and it was not until the name was repeated again, the voice incredulous, slightly raised, that I became aware, a rush of colour to my face, that I had blundered irretrievably, and could not take back my words. 'It's Mrs. Danvers, Madam,' said the voice, 'I'm speaking to you on the house telephone!' "

Men and women alike will experience such an identity crisis, although women are likely to be more keenly aware of it since, usually, they take on their husbands' names. "For a number of months after we were married," Carolyn recounted, "I still thought of myself as Mrs. Chambers and I actually continued to use the name at work. It took me a year to get around to updating my checking account and store charges, partly because of the paperwork involved but partly, I'm sure, because I felt slightly uncomfortable with my new name, like wearing a dress that doesn't quite fit. Mail still arrives for me in my former name. Ken was quite upset by this. At times he was actually jealous of my former husband, even though it was hardly warranted."

If you have lived alone for some time, the need to integrate a new marriage into your image of yourself may run counter to the habit of self-determination that you have cultivated. You may be used to thinking primarily of yourself—"my car" and "my room" and "my house" and "my television set." The transition from mine to ours occurs gradually. Most people furnish their new homes with a potpourri of things—dishes, books, chairs—left over from previous lives. Few can afford to start from scratch. Many things have sentimental value and insist on being kept.

"One of the big problems Ken and I had was sorting out all the possessions that belonged to us, deciding what to keep and what to throw out," Carolyn recalled. Together they had accumulated enough to furnish three homes. "I was touchy about Ken's attitude toward a coffee table and bookcase I owned. I had had them for years and loved them. He kept insisting they were too big for the room, but I felt he didn't want them because they came from my former marriage and former life."

Carolyn suffered with a "love me, love my things" attitude and hence could not be objective about this issue. Their first real argument occurred over the furniture. It was resolved when Ken showed a willingness to have them at the vicarage and only then could Carolyn accept the fact that they simply did not fit in.

The blending of possessions is a tangible expression of the blending of personalities that takes place. One can almost measure the progressive evolution of the new union by the decrease in separateness that characterizes the placement of objects in the home. After a while, his parents' photograph ends up on her dresser and her bracelet, an anniversary present from her former husband, is casually dropped on his bedside table. One rainy afternoon the books are rearranged and, instead of the previous segregation according to original ownership, they now intermingle by subject or without any special order. If there are two copies of the Oxford Unabridged Dictionary, one is given away to a friend or family member.

The process of forming a new "we" is influenced by hidden premises that attach themselves to what being married means. The words themselves—"being married"—spoken aloud or silently, carry powerful emotional overtones. If you were to ask a number of people for immediate responses to them, the list would be long and varied. It would include such phrases as "security," "tied down," "in love," "living together," "trouble," "confinement," "sharing." Summed up, these phrases would testify to the struggle that goes on within each partner between a need for autonomy on the one hand and a desire for fusion on the other.

Consider the meaning of the word "nurturing." Other words, such as "nutrition" and "nourishment," are derived from the same Latin source, which means, basically, "to feed properly." The relationship between two people in a second marriage requires nurturing if it is to grow and remain healthy. The following common-sense rules, if they are carefully observed, will help:

- Both of you must be committed to making the marriage work. In the face of the present widespread disenchantment with marriage, you know there are no guarantees, and so a genuine commitment to each other takes quite a bit of courage.

• You must be able to trust each other, building a confidence that becomes more solid with time because it is proved by experience rather than naïvely assumed. By the time you marry you should know each other well enough to have such a trust, so that when insecurities or disruptions arise, you can spontaneously give each other the benefit of the doubt.

• Mutual confidence can counter the feelings of rejection that inevitably occur from time to time in people who are intimately involved with each other. In a second marriage, having been part of one failed relationship, you will be subject to uncertainties, to moments when you wonder whether your new partner cares enough or respects you as you think he or she should. Resist the temptation to misinterpret meaningless actions, such as forgetting your second anniversary (there are usually so many dates to remember as it is), or small and human insensitivities, such as having too much to drink at a dinner party and falling asleep when you get home when the two of you had planned to make love that night, as evidence of some deep and fundamental rejection. Try not to withdraw or attack in kind. If your wife seems to have grown impatient or indifferent in some way, if your husband forgets to call you while away on a three-day business trip, don't brood about it. Ask if there is anything wrong. And if you are the one being asked, answer directly, truthfully, in the spirit of wanting to keep lines of communication open and untangled.

• Deal openly, though not brutally, with the conflicts that will inevitably arise. If some pattern of behavior in your partner irritates you again and again, do not expect a single discussion to change it. We are not built that way. It takes time for us to modify behavior—being on time for dinner when we have a habit of being late, controlling our tempers when we are used to blowing off quickly, and making plans when we are used to acting spontaneously. Furthermore, we all do better when we are rewarded for our effort than repeatedly castigated for our failure. When there are differences between you and your new spouse that are irreconcilable, perhaps the best thing to do is to agree to disagree.

- Forgive intelligently. If you have been in the wrong, own up to it. Become skillful at making up.

- The closeness you cherish will be broken from time to time since no two people can live in continuing contact with each other without some disruptions. Be prepared to accept such moments for what they are, normal and temporary.

- Love is not a constant state. Stress, distractions, moods such as depression, emotions such as fear or anger, and plain old boredom can creep in to block out or dull that feeling of excitement and intensity that we so commonly associate with "being in love." Don't make the mistake of assuming that you are no longer in love with your partner when you are experiencing such distress, and don't turn to your partner at such a time and say, "I don't think I love you any more." You may find yourself being taken seriously when you don't really mean it.

- A healthy bond involves an "I" and a "Thou," and to form a genuine "We" each of you should have enough personal autonomy. The more you have defined your needs, interest patterns, and expectations of marriage, the more you can form a relationship in which you can give freely to your partner. Too much independence, especially if you are still absorbed in fighting to liberate yourself from some kind of real or imagined bondage, can easily give rise to various forms of behavior that say, in essence, to your partner: "I don't really need you." If competitiveness is added to the picture, the bond can be destroyed in a hurry.

- At the same time, give each other enough space in which to breathe. Privacy enriches closeness. Time alone seems to enhance the value of time together, even as knowing that there is someone, somewhere with whom you are intimately linked in a special way that can make being alone a pleasure rather than a condition of loneliness.

Unfortunately, some of our assumptions make reestablishment of the marriage bond difficult in several ways. We mistakenly assume that love happens, that the new commitment occurs instantaneously. It does not. Love and a sense of commitment grow, and the feeling of "we" grows with it, in time, and reinforces it. However confidently you enter a second marriage, it is unwise to assume that things will run smoothly. The chances are that whatever can go wrong will. Thus one will be better prepared to meet unexpected sources of stress and resolve various problems successfully. As Carolyn and Ken came to understand, the strength of their new relationship derived as much from their ability to settle conflicts and solve dilemmas as from their basic attraction and love for each other.

We have also been encouraged to believe a distorted concept of the nature of the marriage bond itself. Romantic notions suggest that, if you are in love, you should lose yourself in the person whom you love. A little bit at a time, this is true. One should expect a sense of oneness, a mingling together that accompanies a meaningful sexual experience or a strongly emotional moment. Certainly as people live together and grow to understand each other's moods and to anticipate each other's thoughts intuitively, they may well come to feel a special sense of union.

But such a concept is dangerously close to the concept of psychological symbiosis. In symbiotic relationships, one individual is so lost in and dependent upon another that he actually begins to lose his own identity. He feels incomplete without the other. He experiences the merger that marriage presents as an opportunity to blend with a human being who can be all things to him. As one might suspect, since no human being can be everything to anyone, this kind of unequal engagement necessarily leads to an increasing state of helplessness, insecurity, and downright rage within the person who seeks it. Not uncommonly, the partner who has been sought out as the target for such feelings ends up in a position of domination, or, struggling to maintain his own balance, may reject the overtures of the one who tries to develop such total fusion. A union born of symbiosis is better viewed as bondage and bears little resemblance to the kind of union that a good marriage manifests, in which each person can maintain a healthy sense of self and, at the same time, make a genuine commitment to the other.

Some of the premises of the "open marriage" concept also work against the formation of a sound marriage, in particular, the implication that one can commit oneself to a marriage and, at the same time, keep one foot out the door. A forty-year-old man who tried this and lived to regret it recounted: "I'd been divorced for six years. It was a tough adjustment to make, but after a while I came to like it. After I married again, I felt free to go on seeing one of my old girl friends surreptitiously. She knew I was married but didn't object. I felt married and unmarried at the same time. My new wife didn't know at first. But she was a sensitive person and kept telling me that I seemed to be holding back, somehow, from making our marriage a real sharing. Part of me was involved, part wasn't. Maybe I was afraid. Maybe I just wanted my cake and be able to eat it too. Eventually, I told her the truth, half expecting her to accept it. Instead, she was horrified. I promised to end my outside liaison, but as far as she was concerned, it was too late. She said she would never be able to trust me again."

Carolyn and Ken were subject neither to the problem of symbiosis nor the dangers of free-wheeling it in a second marriage. But they were certainly subject to the ordinary conflict that characterizes the gradual forfeiting of total independence in favor of unity. "I liked being in charge of my own day," said Carolyn. "I lived by a timetable of my own making. When Ken and I were first going out together, when the evening was over and each of us went home separately, I missed him, but I also enjoyed that pleasant sense of privacy that I had learned to cherish. After we were married he had to learn that I wanted to be alone, at night, before going to sleep, to read, and that I wasn't rejecting him. I just needed that time for myself."

Ken had similar adjustments to make. Living alone after the death of his wife, he had been able to do things more or less when he wanted to and had had plenty of free time. His children were off in college. He could lead a less organized personal life, having dinner at odd hours, taking two or three days at a time to be all alone to prepare lectures and go over budgets, being there whenever needed to meet the demands of his parishoners. "Now it's different. Carolyn's children live with us. Meals have to be set at certain times. I can't just disappear when I please. In many ways, my work is more of a strain. After many years of being married, my former wife and I had come to terms with the energy I had to expend looking after people. Those pressures were, of course, much greater as the years went on and I had my own parish. But they had become part of our way of life. Now, married again, I had to rebalance the demands of work with my new home life. Carolyn was sensitive to how much time we spent together and not used to being a minister's wife."

Carolyn's sensitivity to rejection was, in fact, stronger than Ken's. This is usually the case when someone has been through a divorce rather than widowed. Most people who have been through one marital failure protect themselves with a layer of defenses against being hurt again. This can produce a certain distance between them and their new partners, a tentativeness that delays the formation of the new bond. Their antennae are usually alert to any sign of indifference, and they are quick to interpret the ordinary ups and downs in the flow of feelings that occur between two people as evidence of not caring.

This fear of rejection is reinforced by the realization of one or both partners that if they could survive divorce once, they could probably do so again, if necessary. This awareness can afford a sense of freedom, but it can also boomerang, accentuating the fear that you could as easily be the one left behind as the one who does the leaving. Even though it is certainly an option, it is a mistake to hold onto the idea of separation as a ready exit in the event that things do not go as expected. It is equally unwise to use the threat of divorce idly in order to discharge anger when faced with the frustrations, disappointments, or disputes that inevitably arise within the close quarters of marriage. One can too easily take these words seriously, for they have a reality to them that they usually do not have for those who have never been through a divorce. Even when they are not implemented, they will undermine the commitment that marriage requires.

The creation of the new "we" is made more difficult when, in contrast to a first marriage, the couple does not have the luxury of spending extended time together, alone, to establish their relationship before others intrude on it.

Carolyn had three children by her former marriage. They were devoted to their father, who had spent every summer at the Cape since the divorce and often had them visit him in Kansas City. None of Ken's four children were living at home; two were married, two others were in college. On the surface, there should have been few problems when the two families joined together. It did not work out that way as a result, in no small measure, of the machinations of Carolyn's former husband.

Although her two daughters accepted the marriage well, Carolyn's son, Jeffrey, then fifteen, resented it. He felt it was a betrayal of his father and went out of his way to be rude to Ken. He would not answer when spoken to, would make sarcastic remarks about the church being full of hypocrites, and, having stayed out late at night and come in at one or two in the morning, as he did sometimes, would refuse to say where he had been. Inasmuch as Jeffrey had kept such hostile feelings hidden before the marriage, his rebelliousness and surly behavior came as a surprise to everyone.

Carolyn was frantic. She tried to talk with him, but he remained belligerent. She began to wonder whether Ken might not have been subtly antagonizing her son. When she suggested this to him, it set off the second major argument in their four months of being married. Slowly she came to recognize that the boy was being spurred on in his rebelliousness by his father, who called less often and had canceled his plans to spend July at the

Cape. In his conversations with Jeff he would ask him how the new living arrangements were working out in such a way as to indicate his hope that they were not. When Jeff described his new room, his father agreed that it sounded pretty small. When the boy indicated that Ken had tried to be pleasant and had asked him to help out around the church, he was met with a sharp and critical remark about Jeff being "used" by his stepfather as "cheap labor."

His mother was torn between her feelings for Ken and her loyalty to the children and a growing sense of futility over trying to create one family out of two. It was Ken's experience, gained from years of counseling, that enabled them to straighten things out. To begin with, he recognized how important it was for the two of them to have time alone together at rather frequent intervals. He arranged for them to travel, whenever possible, to visit friends or simply go to Boston for the weekend or take longer trips once every six months or so by themselves. Carolyn could literally feel the pressure lifting from her as they drove away from the house. He also found a chance to sit down with Jeff and get him to talk about his feelings. Ken carefully pointed out that he knew that he was not Jeff's father and had no intention of taking his father's place or of interfering with his relationship with Jeff or his sisters. Gradually, the boy grew to trust his stepfather. Ken even called Carolyn's former husband and arranged to meet him privately to find out whether or not there was some solution. Being basically well intentioned, Jeff's father began to modify his attitudes and chose to support the marriage in his conversations with the children rather than undermine it.

As the situation with Jeff settled down, Carolyn felt a stronger sense of closeness to Ken. "The first year of our marriage was rougher than I had anticipated. I expected it to be wonderful. There were wonderful moments. But, on the whole, I don't think I can recall so much turmoil since the last years of my marriage and during the divorce."

Over a period of time, with luck and some insight, neither fleeing from closeness nor forcing it, never expecting a second marriage to replicate the best moments of the first, a couple can arrive at an appropriate sense of "we"—one that is more than a matter of language, a superficial "we did this" and "we did that."

The second Christmas she and Ken were married, Carolyn designed a Christmas card; when she wrote, inside, "Carolyn and Kenneth," she lingered over the signature.

It felt right.

9

Some Decided Advantages

People marrying a second time have some decided advantages that improve their chances of making their new marriages successful. They are often less vulnerable to the insecurities and illusions of youth. They are more realistic and have a better idea of what to expect of marriage and can be more objective about the opportunities and hazards that remarriage presents. They are seasoned veterans who have learned the hard way what can destroy a relationship and what is necessary to make it work.

One marriage counselor offered the following observation: "I would prefer not to marry a girl under twenty-four, simply because it's hard to predict what a young woman of twenty-two will be like and want out of life and expect of her husband five years later. If I were a girl, I'd prefer not to marry a man under thirty."

"There are exceptions, but by and large I have noted a substantial personality change in women between ages twenty and twenty-four and in men during their late twenties and early thirties. And this adds more risk to making a permanent commitment." The pattern of growth and change that takes place in each of us is particularly accentuated as we move from the final vestiges of adolescence to a crystallizing of the values, viewpoints, and character traits that are likely to be retained for the rest of our lives.

Younger people who have never been married before can be caught up in a very romantic and unrealistic outlook toward marriage. Sex occupies center stage, pushing the more important issue of compatibility into the wings. Many are still engaged in freeing themselves from the attachments to their original families, a struggle that makes them both more rebellious than they may be later on and, paradoxically, also more dependent, especially if they are not financially self-sufficient.

First marriages are often the special victims of overdependency. Too many young people start out together as couples before they have developed a sufficient sense of self. The young woman who begins a family at a young age is practically as well as emotionally more dependent on her husband than one who has already established herself in some kind of occupation or career. The young man who assumes responsibility for a wife and children while still earning little and having to turn to his parents or hers for supplemental support may, unfortunately, come to regard his marriage as a trap from which he can envision escape only when his last child graduates from college and he himself is ready to collect his Social Security and retirement pension. Many young people unwisely, dangerously, use a first marriage for the primary purpose of providing themselves with a psychological structure to replace home and school.

Too great a dependency on the person you marry or on the marriage itself can generate enough hostility, whether conscious or not, to destroy all affection. Too great a need for someone else can diminish your confidence in yourself and lead to a relationship based more on a fear of emotional deprivation than on a genuine desire for the two of you to be together. Someone who is not a whole person can hardly make a whole commitment to a relationship.

For most, the picture changes in a second marriage. By the time you begin this new relationship you are probably painfully familiar with the risks of undue dependency and have come to acknowledge that a successful marriage insists that you preserve your own individuality while giving freely to your partner.

Second marriages are also less likely to be born out of rebellion. One girl who married at twenty-two, encountering disapproval from her family of the man she was about to marry, was spurred on by their objections not only to defy their judgment but also to reject everything they represented. Her father, a hard-working man who owned a small drugstore in a town about fifty miles west of Milwaukee, represented the antithesis of the exciting life she wanted for herself.

After graduation from college she took a job in Chicago, where she met and married a boy she had known for about a year and had lived with for six months. In contrast to her father he was a lot of fun, although irresponsible. He would often wake her up at two in the morning, after watching the late show on television, and ask her to dress and go out for a drive near the lake. "We were going to make a million," she recalled. "One week it was a new game, like Monopoly, that would sweep the country. The next it was a half a dozen McDonald's franchises. I don't think he held a job for more than two months during the year we were married. I had to cover all our basic expenses. After a while, whenever he'd say let's go out and have a good time, instead of being turned on, I'd feel like slamming the door in his face."

After her divorce she went home to live with her parents for a few months. Unexpectedly, she began to see things in a way she had not before: the closeness, affection, and understanding between her parents, for example. She began to admire their way of life and to respect her father for his devotion to his family. Having previously resented his work as a druggist as something totally lacking in prestige, she now spent hours helping out in the pharmacy and came to realize how well liked and important her father was in their town.

"I had to get something out of my system," she summed up. "I probably shouldn't have married to do it, but you can't rewrite history. Something inside me was driving me to criticize everything that resembled my family's way of life. But once I married, I felt curiously liberated." She had basically married in the middle of an intense and prolonged adolescent crisis. "I had really been quite dependent on my family as a child, in a good way I suppose. Until I was sixteen, I never wanted to leave home. I was desperately homesick the first term in college. Then I began to resent my parents and constructed a long list of grievances to support my attitude." She married again at twenty-eight, under much more auspicious circumstances, when it was no longer necessary for her to go to war with her past in order to be herself.

By the time men and women commit themselves to second marriages they have usually resolved many of these contradictory influences. They have found some answers to such questions as: What do you want to do with yourself? Where do you want to live and how? What kind of a person are you? With what kind of person are you likely to be compatible? What do you expect of married life? One forty-six-year-old man described a common trap waiting for the unrealistic couple in a first marriage: "My former wife wanted a man she could look up to. In her scrapbook she had a photograph that she had cut out of a magazine when she was twelve of a woman sitting at her husband's knee, gazing up at him with admiration as he puffed away on his pipe. In the background there was a fireplace and a large German shepherd dog. We always lived in apartments and never did have either a fireplace or a dog.

"She idealized me. I was her knight in shining armor. But it couldn't last. I was caught up in my own insecurities, a business student going to night school and working during the day and feeling a tremendous distance between what I was and what I wanted to be. And I was very dependent on her. I'd ask her advice as if she were an oracle of some kind. My insecurity made her feel very insecure. As her image of me was extinguished, neither of us could adjust to the change. The next time I'll know whom I'm marrying and, perhaps more important, she'll know me."

A decided advantage for people marrying a second time is that, since they are usually somewhat older, they are likely to be presenting themselves to each other pretty much as they are and as they will remain during the years to come. There are fewer surprises in store for either of them. While some further personality growth is always expected and, ideally, an enriching marital relationship will foster this for both, they are not as likely to find, the second time, that they have committed themselves to a stranger or are one themselves.

Patterns of behavior and attitudes are more firmly established, for better or worse. Personality traits that reflect stability and a capacity to engage in an enduring bond of marriage are easier to recognize. So, too, are those traits that reflect instability. While it is true that many people become emotionally disturbed precisely because they are married to people who are cruel and insensitive, it is also true that many marriages are devastated by certain psychological disorders which, however treatable, often have important genetic and biological roots. Some of these conditions do not manifest themselves until a person is in his or her late twenties or early thirties. Even then they may be so subtle as to pass for perfectly normal, though obviously troubled, behavior. The first time you marry, if at a young age, these conditions may not have appeared.

Two of the most common psychiatric conditions likely to become apparent after the mid-twenties and having seriously detrimental effects on a marriage are paranoid conditions and borderline states. Those who are paranoid usually feel that someone is out to hurt them or has abused them. They categorically blame all of their unhappiness on others, and since the husband or wife to whom they are married is closest at hand, that person is likely to be the chief target for their distrust and assumed to be the primary cause of their distress. Individuals who are borderline suffer with chronic boredom and inner emptiness. They are subject to rage outbursts that are as confusing for others as they are intense since it is often difficult to understand the cause of the explosion; ordinarily it seems to be triggered by minor disappointments and frustrations. Such people place an endless list of demands on those with whom they are involved and, being quite dependent, expect all their needs to be met. When they are not, as they cannot be, the husband or wife is automatically blamed. The husband-wife relationship is further kept off balance because the borderline personality can shift so rapidly and unpredictably from sweetness and affection to intense hate. If you have been through the experience of being married to someone suffering with either of these conditions, you are not likely to wish a repeat performance. If not, forewarned is forearmed.

Another important advantage for many people marrying again is the experience that directly results from having been married before. They have a much better idea of what marriage involves—the stresses, the challenges—and they are more used to coping with them. They have also learned a good deal about themselves and, even though their former marriages may not have worked out, about the nature of the give and take that marriage requires. They have put illusions aside.

Laura Cannon was thirty-two when she married again to her former husband. "I know it will work this time because we're both different. We've grown up a lot. I've learned, for instance, how to set limits. I know how to make my own feelings and ideas clear."

What she was describing was the change that had taken place in her as a result of her demoralizing first attempt at marriage and the effort she had put into changing herself afterward.

Laura was twenty when she first married John. She was a sensitive girl, desirous of pleasing, almost compulsively accommodating. Her sense of her own strengths and her interests had barely crystallized. She was fresh from the simple world of intramural sports and term papers. Her husband, John, was an attractive, energetic man, eight years her senior. He was very absorbed in himself and his career and still quite involved with his parents. "If you can think of living space as being quantified," Laura recalled, "John occupied about ninety percent of ours and I had the ten percent that was left over."

At first she did not mind, and in fact admired, John's dynamism. But as the years progressed, she found herself plagued with self-doubt. She often felt ignored and sometimes as though she had been flattened by a steam roller.

John was neither abusive or tyrannical. He was just himself, and because Laura could not set any limits on him—in fact, she did not even realize that it was important to do so—they spent much of their time with his friends and his family, and as his independence grew hers diminished until the marriage ended in a series of angry explosions on Laura's part and total bewilderment on John's.

"John was, frankly, just the kind of man I wanted to marry, then and now. I admire him. I trust him. I love him. We lived apart for three years. We both dated but no one seriously. We tried to figure out what went wrong. John grew more and more able to listen and understand other people's viewpoints, mine in particular, while I learned how to express myself once I knew what I wanted to say." One evening John took Laura to see a revival of Noel Coward's *Private Lives*, in which a couple had gone to the point of divorce and remarriage to other people before realizing that what they had wanted all along was to be married to each other, though on different terms. Later that evening, at dinner, John proposed again and Laura happily agreed.

You are likely to carry forward into a second marriage invaluable insights you learned in a first. You may, for instance, have discovered how to love and show it. As one man described, "I came from a cold and emotionally sterile home. My parents lived lives of stony silence. In the early years of my first marriage, my wife complained a lot about my not being demonstrative enough, that I paid too little attention to the small things that count, romantic nuances, thoughtful gestures, things she had been used to in her own family and wanted in our relationship. I tried to change. I succeeded to a large extent. I learned, for example, what a woman means when she says she wants a husband to be gentle and sensitive without giving up any of his masculinity. When my wife died of cancer—she was only thirty-four—the grief was incredibly painful. I felt I could never involve myself with anyone again. But I have married again. What my first wife taught me about loving has become part of me, and my new wife and I are both her beneficiaries."

Second marriages offer a fresh start, and this is precisely what many people need. Released from old resentments and detrimental images of themselves, they can now begin to participate in a new marriage that has no such albatross of negative history hanging onto it. When you married your first husband, he may have been very insecure. This made you anxious; you felt that you could never really count on him. Even though, over the years, he became quite self-confident, you could not replace your original perception and hence the feelings and difficulties that went along with it. With someone else you can allow yourself to feel secure in a way you simply never could with him.

Nor is your family there, either, to haunt you and adversely influence your perceptions the way they may have done the first time. One cannot overemphasize the enormous influence that parents have in molding the impressions that a man or woman may have toward the person they marry. Because a first marriage is a totally new experience and one full of uncertainty, you will be particularly suggestible and, like it or not, quite vulnerable to your parents' attitudes. If your mother repeatedly tells you that your husband is "selfish" or "inconsiderate," you will begin to wonder if she may not be right. Perhaps she is seeing something in him that you do not see. You may resent your mother's intrusion, but, at some level, her comments sink in and affect your own vision. A man whose parents keep asking why he allows himself to be dominated by his wife may well begin to hear her requests as demands and feel a growing need to exert his own will, however unwisely and ill-timed.

Such parental interference is considerably less common in second marriages. Parents seem, on the whole, to grow more tolerant. Sometimes they are simply no longer around. If they do try to disrupt the new marriage, they often find themselves facing, instead of impressionable youngsters, adults who are no longer susceptible to parental pressures and who are more capable of forming independent opinions about the relationship.

A somewhat unusual advantage, but one worth mentioning, involves complex psychological processes. For a few people, their first marriages represent a stage on which to complete a predetermined cycle of behavior that somehow must occur before they can be freed of unconscious determinants and able to engage in a meaningful and valid commitment. Even living together before marriage does not usually resolve this dilemma when it exists, for marriage itself is apparently the necessary psychological vehicle by means of which the inner conflicts are both activated and ultimately resolved. For example, an individual may be compulsively driven to reproduce in his own married life a replica of his parents' relationship. In so doing he may create a marriage totally unsuited to his own needs and temperament. The experience of the first marriage fulfills his compulsion, in the manner of a Greek tragedy, and after it is over he can abandon the unconscious model and be free to find someone else with whom he can be genuinely compatible.

When you marry again you most likely will possess an ingredient critical to success: the will to make it work. Some people feel this may be their last chance to find marital happiness, recognizing that the number of available options is limited. Most are willing to modify their behavior as needed and treat their new partners with greater generosity because, having failed once, they do not want to fail again. This sets the stage for a relationship in which the couple are more willing to make important adjustments. Such determination is vital, for the many advantages that a couple in a second marriage can count on are nonetheless offset by certain special stresses they will have to face.

10

Some Predictable Stresses

In a second marriage the couple has not only to contend with the ordinary stresses that go along with being married. There are new and special pressures, unique to second marriages, and the more you are prepared for them, the better your chances are for success.

You may have been brought up with a strong sense of family unity, for example. When the tensions of your last marriage reached the breaking point, the loss of this sense of unity left you confused and disoriented. You may have consoled yourself with the thought that you have been a good mother or father, devoted to your children. But whether you have custody of the children or only visitation rights, the feeling that you are all part of one family vanishes.

You may hope that, once you marry again, this feeling of family will return. But, of course, it rarely does as such. If the children do not live with you, you go on missing the day-to-day contact with them. Even though they may have accepted your new husband or wife well, and he or she in turn has shown them every consideration—fixing meals, taking them on outings, welcoming them into your new home whenever they wish to come—it is simply a fact that their regular lives proceed invisibly, somewhere else. Breakfast and dinner and coming home after school to rooms that contain the possessions they value, having friends over to play with, talking out problems right away as they arise, asking for help with homework—these were all things that were once an integral part of your life together and that no longer can be. When they do visit it is often playtime. As a single man or woman and, later, married again, you are continually concerned with how to make them feel comfortable with you. You entertain them under conditions that are more like a trip to Disneyland than the atmosphere of home. You worry about trying to discipline their behavior or even having an argument with them when they will be going home at the end of the weekend and you won't see them for two weeks or more. You cannot help but be painfully aware of this fragmentation and disappointed that remarriage has only partially solved it.

If they happen to live with you, you often feel as if you have to be both mother and father to them at times, if not all the time. You may have hoped that they would form a relationship with the man or woman you have married that resembles a child-parent relationship, only to find that reality objects. Your new partner may not be able to assume such an attitude or responsibility, or may not care to. Their real father or mother may object and with good reason. In moments of crisis, the children may state, emphatically, "You're not my father" or "You're not my mother." And somewhere out there is someone else who indeed is.

Joining forces with this lack of cohesiveness, time becomes your enemy. Because there are only so many hours in the day and so many weeks in the year, it is now not feasible for you to give as much time to your plural families, your work and your new life together as a couple as you were able to do when there was only one family to account for. You may begin to feel that you are squeezing everyone and everything in and that someone is always being short-changed. You feel guilty about it but helpless to change it. "One weekend we had my kids over for dinner on Friday night," one man described. "There's a big age difference between my youngsters and my wife's, so Saturday we took her little girls to the zoo. Saturday evening we spent with her parents. Sunday we drove out to the country to see my mother in the nursing home. I don't think we were alone together for more than two hours all weekend."

This time problem can be especially severe if the second marriage takes place at an age when either the husband or wife or both are near the peak of their careers. A woman, for instance, at the age of thirty-eight who may have just been promoted to a position as senior editor of a national magazine finds that her job now requires her to travel extensively. If her husband is starting his own business or has just been made a partner in a professional group, putting him under the pressure of more work and longer hours, they will find, at the very moment when personal demands on their time are about to increase, that there is less time than ever to devote to them.

One must recognize and acknowledge that the quality of the time spent together, as a couple and as a family, must be regarded as more important than the quantity. There is less opportunity to live a totally spontaneous kind of life, or one that can be allowed to drift along. Planning becomes essential. A couple must decide together how they wish to divide their time and their energies among the many people who want and need them and then create a strategy to meet these demands. It may, sometimes, resemble the tactics of a military campaign as they pore over road maps and estimate distances so that, for example, it is possible to incorporate a visit to one's parents with an expedition to a state park for a picnic with the children in a single afternoon.

Above all, the couple must make time to be together alone. This may consist of anything from reserving evenings for dinner together at favorite restaurants, a weekend in a small inn in Vermont, or a charter trip to Cancun in the winter. This may not always be easy to arrange, for there will usually be someone to propose an alternative demand. Nonetheless, the policy of private time with each other must be adhered to in order to protect the integrity of the new relationship.

One must also forfeit the dream, however pleasant, that a new family will be the same as the old one. It cannot be. You can overcome the sense of fragmentation by breaking away from the traditional assumption of a family as being, by definition, under the same roof or in the same neighborhood and developing the idea of a family being bound together by invisible ties rather than only tangible ones. You may as well, for this is a concept with which you will have to become comfortable anyway, once your children have grown and gone.

Another important source of stress for the newly remarried is the fact that there is no way the mind can completely discard the impressions formed over years of a former marriage, no matter how it ended. The presence of such recollections can give you a sense of disconnectedness, discontinuity, as if your life had been chopped up into segments. Memories of holidays and doing things together and once cherished, intimate moments are guaranteed to break through into consciousness from time to time, like souvenirs sitting on tabletops, reminding, threatening in a dozen ways to throw off balance your orientation to time and place.

It is tempting to compare your present marriage with your former one. When the comparison is favorable, of course, it can only serve to strengthen your commitment to the new marriage. But when it is not, it can delay or weaken that commitment. It is one thing if your new marriage is clearly not as satisfactory as your last one. It is quite another—and quite dangerous—to take a set of conditions out of context, magnify them, and allow them to serve as a potential source of unnecessary unhappiness. A thirty-five-year-old woman compared her second marriage to her first with curious regret, even though it was a far more fulfilling one for her in many ways. "My former husband and I made all our financial decisions jointly. We invested money in stocks only after we talked about it together. I knew exactly where the money was at all times. My present husband thinks that's unnecessary. He considers the handling of money his business. He gives me a good allowance to run the house and take care of my own needs. He doesn't even mind absorbing the cost of my children, since their father pays nothing for them. But I resent his attitude and wish he were more like my ex-husband and this can become a major source of friction between us."

By now you should have learned that no relationship is perfect, although, since this is your second marriage, you may hope and unrealistically expect that this time it will be. New husbands or wives, however better suited to each other, will inevitably fail to live up to at least one admirable characteristic that former ones possessed: They may have a better sense of humor but not be as willing to spend time with in-laws; they may be more responsible with money but without as good a sense of humor; they may be sexually more exciting but also more temperamental and irresponsible with money. In any event, it is a mistake to focus unduly on those differences and to attempt to convert your new partner into an improved replica of your former one.

Remnants of a former marriage not only endure, quietly filed in your memory. They often appear in behavior in ways that can jeopardize your new relationship. Jealousy, for example, is an especially sensitive issue in a second marriage. You may easily wonder whether your new husband or wife still has a lingering attachment to a former spouse. And what about life between marriages? Were relationships formed during that period that he or she found more fulfilling than yours? Especially when one or both of you had an affair during your former marriages and even more so if that affair was with each other, either of you may wonder whether the bonds of marriage are strong enough to keep the other from doing the same thing again.

A certain amount of jealousy is healthy; it shows that you care or that the person to whom you are married cares and finds you sexually and emotionally desirable. The total absence of any jealousy often betrays either a naïveté or an insufficient degree of involvement. When it is too intense, however, it will cause trouble because the inherent distrust it communicates makes the sense of security and commitment that marriage requires difficult to establish or maintain. The insecurity that jealousy often stems from and, in turn, reinforces raises two questions: First, is there or might there be someone else the other person may care about in such a way as to interfere with the relationship? And, secondly, does your partner really love you at all?

While jealousy is frequently a consequence and carry-over from the experience of having been betrayed in a previous marriage, or a reflection of the individual's own guilt at having been the betrayor, it can also originate in a deeper and more central fear of being unloved or rejected. Whatever its source and assuming that you are dealing with jealousy that is not of pathological degree, there are certain principles to follow to reduce its potentially destructive impact on your new marriage.

First, do not regard any and all forms of jealousy as a sign of distrust. Some jealousy is normal and only shows that you or the person you love cares enough to be jealous. If it is both inappropriate and troublesome, do not act out against it, defiantly and needlessly aggravating it because you feel your partner's jealousy is an insult to your honesty. Rather, knowing that it represents a special insecurity, try to assuage it with reassuring words and loving actions. And, if that is not enough, try to talk it out—seeing if it is superimposed, for example, from a first marriage (where it may have been justified) onto the second (where it is not)—and remove it from the relationship so that a healthy sense of confidence in each other can replace it. If you are the one who is experiencing jealousy, you may have to make a conscious effort to control your behavior so that you do not become irrationally possessive or needlessly provocative, thus driving a wedge between yourself and your new partner. Of course, if you have good reason for distrust, then you may have to reconsider the soundness of your new marriage and ask yourself whether or not it should continue.

Another source of stress that is often intensified in a second marriage is financial, or, as Joel Grey chants in *Cabaret*, "Money, money/ Money, money"—giving it all the sensual, powerful, and evil aura it can possess. Money does more than make the world go round. Whenever the issue of money is introduced into a human relationship, the nature of that relationship invariably changes.

Marriage, divorce, and remarriage are no exception. As one man described, "I moved to the West Coast to avoid going to jail when there way no way I could pay the amount of alimony the court awarded my wife. She kept after me, upping the ante, and even had an arrest notice out for me in New York. There was no way I could see my children. I've married again. I have a new family. They changed the law, sure, but now it's too late to go back and pick up the ties to my children."

The terms of many divorce settlements endure to haunt and disrupt second marriages. While some are arrived at amicably, most are not. To begin with, there is much less money to go around. If a man's income is, say, $28,000, and he is expected to pay his former wife half that amount in alimony and child support, it leaves him only $14,000 before taxes to live on and marry again. Alimony is tax deductible; child support is not. His former wife, unless she is employed, must also adjust her standard of living downward. Moreover, if she marries again, she loses her alimony payments. The effect of new court rulings, in which men may be awarded support for themselves and for the children whom they may be given custody of, cannot really be fully evaluated as yet. In any event, a new marriage will be economically restricted and even more tightly so if the new couple intends to have children themselves.

For one man, by no means an atypical case, it cost a summer cottage, half of his suburban home in Bergen County, New Jersey, and 40 percent of his net income for him to liberate himself from his wife. Having been proud of his material accomplishments, Don Franklin found the idea of lowering his standard of living unpleasant, to say the least. "Helen and I had a big house in Ridgewood. Our savings account had nearly sixty thousand dollars in it. I worked for Helen's uncle, as a salesman in his printing business, and made forty-five thousand a year. He didn't take kindly to our divorce, so I had to quit. My new job pays me a little less and Helen takes a big chunk out of that for herself and our three children. My new wife, Alice, has a little girl, seven. Alice works as a stock analyst on Wall Street, making about twenty-eight thousand, more than I end up with. That's how we survive. Her ex-husband lives in Europe and gives her nothing to support the little girl. We now live in an apartment in a brownstone in Brooklyn and sometimes I sit in the living room, looking out at the emaciated plants that pass for a garden and remember the swimming pool and our two cars and the membership in the tennis club and I feel like a failure."

Don was painfully aware of the fact that Alice was no less affected than he by their economic problems. The fact that a substantial amount of money was being mailed out every month to Helen periodically irritated her, especially when he had to take out a loan to meet some special purchase, such as a new piece of furniture, or when bills would run for two or three months without being paid. Receiving dunning letters and being in debt became a way of life. There was never enough to create the kind of home either of them wanted. They talked of having a child together and wanted one, but they felt unable to afford it.

"One of our worst fights occurred when Alice found the check I had made out to Helen on the table in the front hall, tore it in half and left it there. I was furious, partly because I hated paying it myself. Alice became hysterical, crying, accusing me of putting my children first before our life together. I became defensive and moralistic, saying I had a responsibility to them. It settled down quickly, but even though she continued to be pleasant to them whenever they visited, when they weren't around she would occasionally make sarcastic remarks about 'handouts' and insisted on calling my attention to what she perceived as their effort to manipulate me into giving more money than the separation agreement called for."

Millions of people grade themselves by money, degrade themselves with it, want it, despise it, use it to control others, depend on it as a source of psychological security and destroy otherwise satisfactory marriages because of it. You may have been burned during your previous divorce, and, not wanting to go through the same thing again, you ask for a prenuptial agreement that will cover financial matters in case things do not work out. By so doing, however, you risk putting an obstacle in the way of the trust that is part of the marriage commitment. On the other hand, you may want to get married so much that you ignore the whole subject of money, never stopping to figure out whether your situation can support another marriage and underestimating the potential problems that can emerge if finances are not given their proper due. Money may symbolize independence, and during the period between marriages you may have enjoyed being your own person with your own checking and savings accounts and total control over your expenditures. Thus, when you marry again, the need to share resources may become a battlefield on which the fight to preserve one's freedom takes place.

If you can, it is best to start out a new marriage by removing the emotional and symbolic meaning that you may always have placed in dollars and cents. It's not easy. If money has been a token of your masculinity, for example, and your new wife happens to earn more than you do and your marriage requires her contribution to remain solvent, you will have to get rid of the premise that equates your value as a person with the amount you give to the running of the household and instead root your self-esteem in something less tangible and, frankly, more authentic. If your husband has payments to make to a family by his previous marriage and they are not exorbitant, you will have to accept these with the same fatalism with which you accept income and property taxes, and eventually not even consider this money in the budget that you establish for yourselves.

Another stress to a second marriage, one that is more subtle than financial conflicts, is the problem of trying to incorporate into your new marriage remnants of your former life that really do not fit. The blueprints you followed in a former marriage were not only the expression of your own interests and those of your partner, but they were also the product of the blending of personalities that being married produced. Between marriages, you have created another style of life. Now, married again, you are engaged in establishing one suited to yourself and your new partner together. It is a mistake to try to begin a second marriage rigidly holding on to those aspects of your former marriage that you liked and getting rid of those that you did not. Better to pretend that you have never been married before and in this way come to discover that there are undeveloped interests that each of you have that will fit together nicely. In your previous marriage you may have enjoyed entertaining friends extensively. You also enjoyed traveling, but your former partner did not, so you seldom did. In your new marriage you find that although travel is an important, shared interest and so becomes a major activity, your new partner prefers less of a social life, one restricted to the company of a few close friends. You may recall old parties wistfully at times, but better to let them fade from memory than to try to force that element of another life into a relationship in which it does not belong.

This does not mean that there will not be characteristics that resemble or are even the same as before. You may enjoy the same books, the same music, the same films. But if you do, it is still best to let the reminiscences fade and settle into the new marriage with a little of the wonderment that goes along with any new discovery.

And as you let go of the past in favor of the present, you will also learn to deal with a specter that hovers above most second marriages, adding to the stress you have to cope with—guilt, whether justifiable or unwarranted.

11

What to Do about Guilt

It may be hard to believe, in a society in which people have become so self-oriented, that such a thing as guilt still survives. As one prohibition after another has been lifted and we have been encouraged to think that we should do whatever we please whenever we want, the word "guilt" has become singularly absent from our vocabularies. Ask people today, four decades after the full impact of Freudian theory on the United States, how they feel about guilt. Many would find it a neurotic and unhealthy emotion to be ignored or, preferably, avoided entirely.

Trying to annihilate the phenomenon of guilt has not dispensed with it at all but merely driven it underground, where it makes us considerably more vulnerable to its influence. At the same time, we have made it harder for ourselves to resolve our own guilt or listen to it as an important signal that warns us we may be engaged in a pattern of destructive behavior.

Guilt is an uncomfortable, distressing, at times quite painful feeling associated with one's failure to live up to certain expectations placed on oneself. Its target is self-esteem. The natural consequence of feeling guilty is to be unhappy, depressed, think less of ourselves than we care to, and expect some kind of retribution or punishment to be exacted from us. Because of this, it also makes us feel afraid.

Being a permissive society, one that prefers not to set limits on behavior, we have tried to deal with the problem of guilt by removing the punishment aspect and the idea of atonement. Thus we have created a situation in which when we feel guilty we are likely to be left hanging with our discomfort, or, since no one else will call us to task, we tend to seek ways to expiate our guilt by punishing ourselves.

The problem of guilt is a major one for people entering second marriages. Even a widow or widower will wonder, at times, whether rechanneling love from someone who has died to someone new is a form of disloyalty. If, after a person has survived a divorce and is about to remarry, one of his children should become ill, mentally or physically, he may be assailed by the thought that the pursuit of his own happiness has somehow led to tragedy for one of his own children.

It is important, therefore, if you are marrying again to crystallize your ideas about guilt, understand its ramifications and the potential harm it can do to your new relationship if it is not properly resolved.

One of the important problems connected with guilt is that it is often hard to recognize, and even when you know it is guilt you feel it may be difficult to spot its origins. You may feel little guilt over the break-up of a clearly unworkable marriage but considerably more over the break-up of a home and its effect on the children. When one ends a marriage that is not so obviously problematic, however, the likelihood of guilt is greater and the probability that it will influence a new marriage is high. Since guilt compromises self-respect, it can make you feel unloved, even rejected, and this feeling, in turn, can affect your perception of an event or remark so that it is interpreted to confirm your low self-esteem. It is a quick and easy leap from an "I don't like myself" position to "You don't like me" and the conclusion that the marriage isn't working.

A fifty-one-year-old man, married to his second wife, thirty-eight, described his bewilderment with her behavior this way. "Everything seemed fine until we actually married and lived together. Then, funny statements would creep into her conversation, like how much she had to put up with in me and how I took her for granted and abused her. I tried to appeal to reason. I recall sitting down one evening and making out a list of her grievances and answers to each one, and I read it to her and all she said was that it didn't prove a thing. She kept insisting that I put everyone else in my life first, my children, my work. It got so bad that whenever she would look sad or unhappy, instead of being able to be comforting, as I had at first, I found myself getting furious inside, because I felt that her look was an accusing one. I'd ask her to talk it out. She'd refuse, or if she did say anything, she always referred to something I had done or hadn't done to upset her." Only through psychological counseling was it possible to identify for this couple that the misperceptions that nearly destroyed their relationship were rooted in the wife's unrecognized sense of guilt. Having married the first time on the rebound, she had brought little to her first marriage other than a bland liking for, and admiration of, her husband. Her former husband being very much in love with her and committed to the marriage, found the disequilibrium unbearable, and the divorce had left him resentful and bitterly unhappy. She, in turn, was left with a great deal of guilt over being the cause of that unhappiness.

The sources of guilt, as psychoanalytic theory has proposed, can also be in neurotic conflict. A man or woman may feel, for example, that they have no right to find any more satisfaction in life than their parents did. If their parents had an unhappy marriage, they may feel compelled to do likewise. Sometimes, by choosing unwisely, they can guarantee themselves a relationship that makes them miserable. But if, by chance, they choose well, they can, motivated by guilt and the sense of undeservedness that goes along with it, turn a potentially good marriage into a shambles.

But there is a more existential source of guilt as well. Throughout man's history certain modes of behavior have served us well; others have threatened our survival. In order to accentuate that which is good for us and warn us against actions that are potentially dangerous, societies have set up various guidelines for us to follow. These moral codes have changed. In a rather simplistic way we have tended to attribute such standards to particular cultures. Carl Jung, however, in his theory about the collective unconscious, reminded us that there are imprints within the brain cells that carry foward messages from antiquity, messages that have to do with expectations of human behavior intrinsically related to evolution and the continuation of life. Among other things, these messages tell us what it is to be a mother, a father, a husband, a wife, and they deal with such broad concepts as loyalty, trust, generosity, good, evil.

In other words, standards of behavior against which we can measure our own thoughts and actions are not only set up by society but they are also derived from within our very nature. When these are violated we experience guilt. Unfortunately, one of the contemporary problems that we all face is the spirit of "anything goes" that blurs the borders between desirable and undesirable behavior and leads us to assume, falsely, that we can do whatever we want without answering for the consequences. When, in the past, there were better defined expectations, people may have ignored them or acted in spite of them. But at least they did so knowingly, and, if they felt some guilt as a result, they knew that too. When such expectations vanish, however, and we are free of concern about culturally imposed standards, we think that we have solved the problem of self-esteem by eliminating certain yardsticks against which to measure it. Unconsciously, however, in the recesses of our minds, the more existential guidelines still exist, reaching up to cause us unexpected pain and confusion when we do not acknowledge their significance.

One such existential message is that parents should protect the well-being of their children. There is overwhelming evidence that children whose parents are in conflict or have divorced will suffer because of it. No matter how solid the reasons for divorce may be and how ultimately beneficial to the well-being of all involved, including the children, there is no way that a parent can avoid some sense of guilt toward his children.

Don Franklin was a good example of this problem. He had postponed ending his first marriage for some years on account of his children. At the time of his divorce, his older daughter was sixteen, his younger daughter was fourteen, and his son was twelve. Each of them reacted to the divorce differently. Martha, the sixteen-year-old, was quite resentful toward Donald and experienced the separation as if he had seriously injured her mother. For a year afterward she avoided seeing him, using activities with her friends as an excuse. The fourteen-year-old girl, Joan, seemed indifferent, but her school work deteriorated for about a year and she developed a "who cares" attitude toward life. His son, John, was perhaps the most profoundly affected, becoming obviously depressed. The first spring vacation following the divorce Don took his son on a camping trip. In the middle of the night he was awakened by the sound of the boy sobbing in his bunk. He went over to the other side of the cabin, sat on the edge of the bed, and put his arm around the boy's shoulder to comfort him. "Why can't I live with you, Dad?" the boy asked. Don felt a terrible sinking feeling and a sense of intense frustration.

Even though he waited four years before marrying again and, during that time, the children seemed to have rebounded from their reactions to the divorce, Don could not free himself from the feeling that they had suffered because of what he had done. "When I thought of it being my fault, I felt guilty," he recounted. "When I considered it my former wife's fault, I felt a kind of welling up of fury at her for not having been a different kind of person."

His sense of guilt led to a continuing state of mild depression. He was, therefore, quite sensitive to criticism, which made it harder for him to deal with the directness of his new wife, Alice. This mood also reinforced his jealously and feelings of insecurity about their relationship. If, after a visit with the children, things did not seem all right with them, he would, in characteristic style, become slightly morose and withdraw into the newspaper or the television set, thus upsetting Alice. His vulnerability to and preoccupation with his children was one of the reasons she had become so angry about the money that he had to send to Helen for support.

"You can't deny them anything," Alice would say, and Don would reply angrily, "You couldn't possibly understand the problem I have to deal with." He was unable to appreciate fully the extent to which Alice put herself out for his children. Nothing he himself did ever seemed to be enough. If his son, now sixteen, were to call on the phone on Friday and ask if he were free to do something with him that weekend, Don could never say no directly, even if he and Alice had made other plans that could in no way be changed. Instead he would say, "Why don't you call me in the morning and we'll see what we can do." When the boy would call the next morning, Don would hesitantly admit that he could not be available and would have to see his son another time. The silence on the other end of the phone made Don feel awful, and the thought of having disappointed the boy made him irritable. Not infrequently, after an episode such as this, he and Alice might see some friends and he would have a little too much to drink and end up arguing about politics or people, embarrassing both her and himself. When his twenty-year-old daughter, Martha, coldly informed him that she needed a car for college and implied that if he did not get her one she might just not bother contacting him again for some while, he promptly acquiesced and borrowed the money to buy her a used one. Alice was furious.

The guilt that people who marry a second time feel toward the children they have by a previous marriage can have a positive influence, promoting a healthy concern for those children and motivating constructive efforts to see to it that they do not suffer any more than they have to because of events over which they have had no control.

But, at the same time, many people who experience such guilt only further compound their own difficulties as well as those of their children by not appreciating how strongly it is governing their actions. Not only can guilt drive a wedge between the couple trying to build a new life together, but it can also have a detrimental effect on the growth and development of the children themselves.

By avoiding or postponing confrontations in which he would necessarily have to disappoint his son, Don was only intensifying the boy's feelings of rejection and susceptibility to disappointment and paradoxically making him more dependent on his father than a teenage boy should normally be. By giving in to the demands of his daughter, Martha, he was only encouraging her to believe that the best way to get what she wanted was to threaten the person she wanted something from with the withdrawal of her love and attention.

Here again Alice proved to be most helpful. Because she did not basically resent the presence of his children in their life and because she could, at the same time, be quite objective with regard to the interactions that took place between Don and his children, she was able to gradually move him away from the permissiveness and overindulgence that characterized his attitude and show him that a more definitive approach to them, one in which he would combine caring with the setting of realistic limits, would not only make him feel more comfortable but would also permit his children to gain the independence that their adolescent years demanded of them.

The recognition and handling of guilt, then, is a critical factor in determining the success of a second marriage. Assuming that it is not of neurotic origins, in which case some kind of therapy is clearly in order, the guilt that most men and women who are married again must face and overcome can usually be resolved by observing these guidelines:

- Accept the fact that the better things go for you, the more likely you will be to be subject to some degree of guilt. It is a universal part of the human condition to feel that, in some way, we do not deserve the good things that come our way.

• Accept, as well, the fact that no matter how your former marriage ended or regardless of the reasons for its ending, you will experience divorce as a failure for which you are, in some way, at least partially responsible. Indulging in self-righteousness and blaming the other person is no solution if this prevents you from appreciating your own contributions to the problem. Your feelings of culpability will be intensified if there are children involved, especially if they have been adversely affected by what has happened.

• Watch out for the subterranean consequences of guilt, particularly when you have not been dealing with it directly. It can make you more sensitive to rejection, put you too much on the defensive, lead to unnecessary quarreling, make you feel depressed and out of sorts, and disrupt your adjustment to a new marriage unless and until it is settled.

• Accept your limits. Genuine humility is an important antidote for guilt. It works this way. First, because you can accept the responsibility for your past actions, you can experience regret for those actions that deserve regret and make amends where amends are appropriate and can be made. Secondly, you can begin to appraise more intelligently the complex forces that have gone into making you what you are today. You may have married the first time at too young an age and for somewhat dubious reasons, such as the desire to escape an unpleasant situation in your home. Being the kind of person who could not express your emotions directly, you may have unwittingly expressed them through destructive behavior such as carrying on an affair to hurt your former husband or wife. Circumstances may have conspired to make the man or woman whom you are now married to enter your life at precisely that time when your former marriage was at its lowest ebb. The person who is dominated by guilt is commonly the one who has the illusion that he or she is in complete control of their life. Better to combine a sense of your own influence with an appreciation of the role fate or destiny plays in the lives of each of us.

• Try not to spend too much of your time and energy in an effort to think well of yourself. Whatever you have done wrong, know that you share your weakness with everyone else no matter what their personal life seems to be like on the surface. Do not compare yourself with those whose marriages have held together or even those whose marriages are working out quite well. You can deal with life only on the terms that life has given you.

• Do not allow guilt to influence your behavior adversely. Many people tend to dwell on their guilty feelings. This rarely leads to solutions. In fact, it is inherently anticreative, for the best way to solve most problems is to gain some distance from them and be able to reappraise them in a new light later on. It is also important not to allow others to manipulate or control you by getting a handle on your sense of guilt and using this power to get you to do things that are neither in your own self-interest nor in the interest of your new marriage. Former wives and children by previous marriages may learn that by saying to you, "Look what you have done to me" and showing you a few scars they can get what they want from you, or at least prevent you from finding happiness in your present relationship.

• Above all, do not let your sense of guilt from the past transfer itself to your present and turn your new marriage into a cauldron of suffering, blame, and misunderstanding.

• Finally, keep in mind the constructive purposes of guilt. It is a warning signal that can keep you from doing things that might destroy what you have built up for yourself. The issue of marital fidelity is a good illustration, for even though contemporary standards would encourage you to doubt its relevance to marriage and make you believe that a good affair may actually make your new marriage work better, deep inside you is a voice that whispers, "Maybe not." A deeply etched imprint in the brain, carried forward genetically and inscribed with a dictum from the collective unconscious, may be telling you that loyalty and honesty are essential ingredients in marriage and that, popular opinions to the contrary, certain essentials of human nature and human relationships have not changed that much over the centuries.

12

Hauntings

A James Thurber cartoon shows a man identifying a woman crouched on top of his bookcase as his first wife, suggesting how former husbands and wives may literally haunt a new life, exerting an ongoing and frequently disruptive influence.

Of course, if you were married only a brief time and had no children together, your first partner will probably disappear from your life. You may remain friends, but more often you will have little or no contact with each other as the years pass. If you do happen to meet, at a party or an airport, your encounter may resemble the chance meeting of casual acquaintances.

If, however, you have been married for some time, and especially if there are children your relationship will most likely never really end. The children themselves will remind you, by a physical resemblance, a gesture, a way of talking, of the person you once shared a life with.

And while the nature of the residual relationship with a former spouse can vary greatly, most seem to fall into a few typical patterns. You may find, most enviable of all, that you and your former husband or wife have remained friends throughout; or that, although you were at one time enemies, you have regained some respect and liking for each other and so have entered a more comfortable relationship; or unfortunately, that, you are perpetually at odds with each other.

If the third circumstance applies, you should formulate a kind of foreign policy of conduct toward a former husband or wife. Your ultimate purpose is fourfold:

- To prevent the former partner from draining either your emotional or material resources.

- To prevent your relationship with your former husband or wife from having a detrimental influence on your new marriage.

- To keep any ongoing hostilities or manipulations from hurting your children.

- To try, if possible, to restore or maintain some semblance of respect between you and the person you once shared a marriage with.

How can you accomplish these ends? There are certain time-worn principles, derived from painful experience, you should observe.

If the financial or legal structure that was drawn up is clearly inequitable and hence repeatedly provocative—a husband paying a punitive amount of alimony or a wife never knowing from month to month whether the money to which she is entitled will be coming—try to get this straightened out. Granted, it is not easy; however, an arrangement that was set up in anger may lend itself to being improved when tempers cool and resentment subsides.

If there are ongoing hostilities, however they show up—through critical and unfair remarks made to children, by way of total noncommunication, by routine calls to discuss some simple matter such as visitation arrangements that end in bickering and hanging up—consider two things. First, what is the source of the hostility? And secondly, what can you do to reduce it, or at least keep it contained? The origins will determine, in no small part, the solutions.

If the hostility you encounter from a former husband or wife is rooted in insecurity (because the world that he or she depended on has been rudely shattered) or in vindictiveness (because of feelings of rejection), time is on your side. As your former partner settles down, creates a new life, becomes accustomed to being apart from you, and finds new interests, the chances are good that reasonable communication and some of the old respect for each other will return. In such a case, try to handle your contact with your former mate with some degree of compassion and tolerance. Stay in touch. Avoid arguments. Do not respond in kind to provocations.

If the hostility toward you stems from deeper sources, your strategy will have to be quite different. It is one thing to have had a number of good years together and then find your marriage falling apart. It is quite another to have been engaged in arguments, long days of silence, power struggles and other forms of warfare throughout your marriage. If what has happened since your divorce and remarriage is only a continuation of what was going on for years before, there is little reason to expect it to change. Here, as a rule, the less contact you have with each other the better. With no resolution possible, it is pointless to go out of your way to please or accommodate. Moreover, you may have to use quite a bit of firmness and ingenuity to set limits on your former partner's behavior, refusing to take the bait and be stirred up by provocative remarks, insisting that he or she live up to the terms of your separation agreement. Sometimes the best thing to do is simply be unavailable when he or she tries to reach you on the phone.

This policy of noninvolvement is especially important if your former husband or wife is paranoid—not in the sense of having full-blown delusions but showing a tendency to distort what you say and how you behave. One cannot reason with such unreason, and if you attempt to do so, you will find yourself gradually being reduced to a state of confused and angry immobility.

Even when there is not such open combat, there are other negative maneuvers that call for different precautions. A former husband or wife may, for example, reach out in a dependent way, looking for emotional support and asking for guidance. By all means offer it, but be careful not to encourage the kind of involvement that leads to undesirable consequences. There are two common dangers: First, you may delay your former partner's development of a life of his or her own. Secondly, you may compromise your relationship with your new partner.

It is essential for those in a second marriage to behave in such a way as to make it eminently clear that the new relationship comes first.

Part of your commitment to your new marital partner includes a willingness to help him or her cope successfully with a former mate. If indicated, you should help your husband or wife set intelligent limits on the disturbing behavior of a former partner. Be careful not to encourage any petty vindictiveness or anger that will only aggravate the situation. It is far more constructive to encourage an end to the unnecessary guilt that is all too common after divorce. Try not to engage in misplaced jealousy; remember, the chances are excellent that if your new husband or wife still had any real feelings of love left toward a former partner, he or she would still be living with them, or at least the two of you would not be married. If there were good years together in a former marriage, as is often the case, there is bound to be some element of affection left and memories of good times together, but this should offer no threat to the current relationship.

All divorces are not bloody, by any means. There may, in fact, be genuine affection and mutual regard. Liz Matthews was twenty-eight when she and her former husband, Sam, were divorced. They had been married for seven years. While Sam was completing his graduate work at Princeton, Liz took care of their two children, both girls, and worked part time as a computer programmer to help pay their expenses. Sam was a good-natured, pleasant man who wanted to write and teach history. Liz was a tall, dark-haired girl with a lively sense of humor and a bachelor's degree *magna cum laude* from Wellesley. She had planned to go to law school.

Liz felt she had made a mistake in marrying Sam almost from the first weeks of their marriage; but feeling that he was such a "nice person" and that marriage should be a permanent commitment, Liz never seriously thought of leaving him. But as the years went on, she felt a growing sense of unhappiness. "I felt trapped, desperate for a different way of life. I felt my resentments toward Sam, which were petty and sometimes very unreasonable, would wreck his career and his own chances for happiness. I could never give him the love he deserved. I could never be fulfilled myself. The night we finally agreed to break up we held onto each other and cried for hours. I had to fight the temptation to go back to him for months afterward."

Then, and in the years that followed, there was no

animosity between Liz and Sam. She went back to school to study law and he went on to a teaching post at the University of North Carolina. Three years later, when Liz was thirty-one, she met and married Arthur Endicott, a forty-year-old lawyer. Arthur was a much more energetic and outgoing man than Sam. Liz found him sexually very attractive. Arthur had been divorced some years earlier, but in contrast to Liz's experience, his had been a very difficult marriage and an even more difficult separation.

"Arthur was so scared by his own experience that he could not understand the fact that Sam and I could have a good relationship. When I suggested that Sam stay with us when he visited the children, Arthur was furious and wanted to know whether I was still in love with Sam." Gradually, however, as Arther came to understand the situation, the two men developed a good rapport.

Sam never married again. The success he attained in his work served to relieve Liz of her guilt and reinforce her conviction that she had done the right thing for both of them. He was meticulous in sending his child-support checks—Liz had refused alimony—and he visited his children faithfully.

This kind of harmonious relationship is the exception, however, and not the rule. More often the relationship between a former husband and wife is replete with grievances. This is particularly true when one of them has not married again. They remain locked in a complex dependency-hate interaction with each other, the former partner doing whatever he or she can to undermine or throw lye into the new marriage the other one is trying to establish. There are two prevalent motives for such behavior. The first is simply revenge, where the former partner is trying to obtain retribution for the real or imagined rejection that he or she has experienced. The second is resentment, stemming from the loss of the security that both marriage and the former partner once provided.

Sarah, Arthur Endicott's former wife, was a case in point—an ongoing problem and a chronic irritant for both Arthur and Liz. "When Sarah and I were married," Arthur described, "she was extremely dependent on me. She wanted me to handle the money. She would not drive a car. I was expected to help solve all her family's problems and that was no small undertaking. At the same time, she often treated me like one of the children, telling me to do this or that, criticizing me whenever I didn't do exactly what she wanted the way she wanted it done. For years I gave in, but at the end, when I didn't, we were always fighting and arguing."

Arthur's divorce had been filled with confusion and animosity. Sarah's attorneys managed to tie up most of his assets for over a year. "I needed some of them to live on. But they wouldn't listen to reason," Arthur recalled. "The house was our major asset, worth about eighty thousand dollars at the time. We had another thirty thousand dollars in stocks and savings, all in joint name. I offered to split it down the middle, which is how it was eventually settled. But they wanted it all. It took countless meetings with lawyers and a couple of court appearances before I could get a cent."

The week after Liz and Arthur were married, Sarah sent Liz a malicious note, expressing her interest in the new marriage and the hope that Liz would eventually come to appreciate Arthur's true character. Liz tore it up without showing it to Arthur. But she grew increasingly impatient with Arthur's futile efforts to placate Sarah. "The nicer you are," she told him, "the worse she gets." Which, in fact, seemed to be the case. Arthur, for example, would arrange to be prompt when he would go to pick up his children for a weekend. Sarah would keep him waiting but not permit him in the house. Once, when he was half an hour late, she took off with the children to a friend's house for the rest of the afternoon and, later on the telephone, scathingly accused him of "not caring enough to be on time."

Over the months Liz began to feel the strain. "She only upsets you when you talk to her. Why don't you just stop?" she suggested. Arthur replied, "What choice do I have? I have to try to make things work for the children's sake." Finally, when Liz pleaded, "You are going to have to do something, or you'll wreck our own chances for happiness," Arthur tried a different tactic. At first he found himself losing his temper and shouting at his former wife whenever provoked to do so. But all this accomplished was to reinforce her self-righteousness and give her an opportunity to hang the phone up on him. Once, just as Liz and he were getting ready to go away on a ten-day vacation to Bermuda, he was handed a subpoena by a process server at his office. Sarah was suing him for more child support, having learned of the impending trip through the children. This proved to be the final straw. Arthur now realized that not only was there no point in trying to conciliate and placate Sarah, but his efforts to express his anger had not paid off either. It was time to become really detached. Conversations with Sarah became brief, limited only to the matters at hand. He began to spot maneuvers to move onto controversial topics and resisted them. He might wince inside when Sarah said anything provocative or hurtful, but he would maintain a surface coolness. Predictably enough, as Sarah began to see that he was no longer vulnerable to her manipulations, she made fewer and fewer efforts to disturb either Arthur or Liz.

Such continuing resentment from the person you were

once married to generally means that he or she still has a strong emotional investment in you. Probably still dependent on you, your former spouse is trying to keep the interaction alive in the only way he or she seems to know—by creating situations designed to stir up your hostility. While such warfare is sometimes intentional, more often it is motivated by unconscious conflicts in the former partner, making appeals to reason virtually useless. The best you can do is to try to minimize the impact on you and your new marital partner. Restrict your conversations to essential, practical issues that have to be dealt with—such as the children. It is best not to respond in kind, by getting angry or vindictive, nor to struggle to be accommodating in hopes that by being nice you can change attitudes. Either extreme encourages the continuation of the behavior. If necessary, pretend total detachment. The message you wish to deliver is that your relationship with your former partner is now over. Despite his or her efforts, you must be able to resist feeling guilty or reengaging in squabbles, power struggles, insults or other conflicts that may well have started long before your divorce and have simply continued since.

What should you do if the person you are now married to is confronted with a former partner doing his or her best to cause trouble? Don't add to the stress by fanning the resentment with a "why don't you just tell them where to get off?" attitude. It is equally unwise to harp on your new husband's or wife's vulnerability to the harassments. Because, in theory, you have a little more perspective on the situation, you may be able to shed some constructive light on what is happening and foster the only solution that works: an end to the old relationship.

Many marriages break up on account of severe psychological and behavioral problems. And so, in a second marriage, you may have to face dealing periodically with an emotionally disturbed former husband or wife. One of the most common behavioral problems that you may encounter is a former partner who is an alcoholic.

Jane Miller's former husband, Sid, had been a heavy drinker throughout their marriage. His abusive behavior when drunk was the primary reason for their divorce. Now, fifty, having been married for nearly ten years, she still could not escape the impact of her former husband's drinking. "He'd call up unexpectedly in the middle of the night, drunk, from some bar, and ramble on about how he had been mistreated and misunderstood. When our oldest daughter graduated from high school, he showed up at graduation intoxicated. He embarrassed us all terribly."

Sid had made gestures toward joining Alcoholics Anonymous but never followed through after the first two or three meetings. With his mother dead, his father too old to do much for him, and his one brother having long since made it clear he wanted nothing to do with him, Jane was left to carry the burden.

"We were the only family he had. My new husband was heroic about this. We've had to hospitalize Sid at detox centers to dry him out three times in the last two years. I used to suffer with an awful feeling of responsibility for him. I thought that, somehow, I might have had something to do with his drinking. But I'm free of this now. The reason I can't drop him entirely is because I am really concerned about the influence he might have on the children. If I ran away from it altogether, they'd be the ones to be stuck with him."

If the person you have married is confronted with a similar problem, it is important to be compassionate. At the same time, when your new marriage is being victimized by the problem, you should both encourage and help your partner set firm limits. In Jane Miller's case, with her husband's help, she was able to recognize that no one except her ex-husband himself could solve his drinking problem. She began to keep him at a distance. "For instance," she said, "my husband advised me to tell Sid that if he called us from some bar, we'd hang up on him. We'd do the same if he called drunk. Or if he called in the middle of the night. He tested us out a few times and when we did just what we said we were going to do, he gradually stopped. For the last few months he's called only when sober."

A former husband's or wife's disturbing behavior offers one definite advantage. It serves to remind you, from time to time, and lest you forget, how fortunate you are to be out of that relationship and into a better one. Arthur Endicott confirmed this. "I have to admit that there are times when I forget just how bad things were with Sarah. We did have some good years together. But as soon as she tries one of her bids for attention or revenge, I remember in a hurry."

Many people who are about to marry again are concerned about the impact of remarriage on a former husband or wife. Will it make things worse? Arthur Endicott's former wife's efforts to demoralize him, her appetite for lawsuits and game playing, were certainly spurred on by his marriage to Liz. Liz's attitude toward the possibility of Sam remarrying was quite different, though no less complex. "If Sam were to marry again and make a good choice, I'd be really pleased. That's partly because Arthur and I have a good relationship. Sometimes I worry about Sam, whether's he's lonely, and I feel a bit guilty. However, if I weren't married to Arthur, I might feel differently. The thought of the children having a stepmother would make me apprehensive. Before Arthur and I fell in love, it was a source of security for me to imagine that if anything went wrong, Sam might take me back, and he would. I think that if he had married then, I would have felt a little frightened, maybe even—selfishly—resentful."

How remarriage affects the relationship between a divorced couple depends, in part, on the kind of bond that existed between them during the years of their marriage. The more unhealthy that bond, the more resistant it is to being severed. You must not confuse the positive closeness and sharing found in successful marriages with the negative intense interdependency or competitiveness that characterizes distinctly pathological bonds. By understanding the nature of that negative interaction we can often predict what a former partner will do. As one man observed, "My former wife ran off and married a guy she had known only for six weeks. That was a few months after I remarried. It lasted about three months and then she got a civil annulment. I have no doubt but that it was the result of the same old competitiveness. She couldn't stand the idea of my being married again so she just took off with the nearest man in sight. That's what our life was like before."

If you had some good years together in your former marriage, before things fell apart, the chances are that over a period of time you will rediscover some of the respect and caring you once had toward each other. A second marriage can sometimes actually facilitate such a reconciliation. Most people emerging from a broken marriage are wounded and it takes time for these wounds to heal. With the passing of time and the acquisition of experience come wisdom and objectivity. There is an old medical adage that warns the physician not to hurt the patient while attempting to heal him. The same advice would serve well for those who, now remarried, are searching for a strategy to deal with former husbands and wives. It is important to give both person and past the benefit of the doubt, while, at the same time, making it eminently clear to your new partner that he or she is now the main focus of your love.

13

Thursday's Child Has Far to Go

Some degree of depression is common among children of divorced parents. Ordinarily depression is self-limiting and will clear up within six months or a year. But sometimes it can go on for a much longer period of time, especially when unrecognized or repeatedly aggravated by circumstances or other people. Depression may manifest itself in obvious ways: sleeplessness at night, loneliness and crying, a pulling away from ordinary interests, activities, and friends. In children, however, depression is not always so apparent. Their reaction to change and loss often shows up in behavior rather than mood, so that, instead of seeming sad, children may engage in repeated actions that irritate and provoke parents and teachers. Younger children might smear paint on the walls of the kitchen; older ones might talk back rudely to teachers in the classroom. Characteristically, the aberrant behavior persists in spite of retaliatory punishment. Depressed children also often have a low estimate of their own abilities. A child who previously may have shown considerable academic or athletic ability might gradually slide back to a level of competence well below his usual one and resist any efforts to help him improve.

The impact that divorce has on children is determined by their age. Very young children, those under the age of four, do not seem as significantly affected as older ones. Children between the ages of four and eleven react strongly to the loss of family structure. Those in their early and mid-teens are working to achieve appropriate independence, and divorce threatens to impede this movement. It is important, therefore, to treat each age group somewhat differently. Two cardinal rules should be observed. First, when children under twelve are involved, it is essential to restore structure and a sense of security as quickly as possible and do whatever can be done to renew the child's confidence in the dependability of his or her parents. Secondly, when the children are in their adolescence, it is important to protect and not block their growth toward self-identification and separation from the family. Doing so requires that neither parent lean on them, making them feel, for example, that they need to supply the love and companionship that their divorced parent now lacks. It also means that the parents should refrain from using children as pawns in a continuing adult battle to hurt each other or to force the child into a position of divided loyalty. Again, this ideal is seldom achieved.

The children of divorced couples who continue battling soon become uniquely skilled in the art of manipulation. Sensing intuitively their parents' weak points, they can reinforce the already existing animosity and make one or both parents feel guilty enough to supply additional time, money, or attention. Because such children are often more vulnerable to disappointment and more easily frustrated when they do not get what they want or need, they may readily find that successful manipulation of their parents puts them in control and averts such disappointment.

It is important to counter a child's tendency to maneuver parents in this way. The most effective solution lies in restoring some degree of constructive communication between the parents so that they can provide a consistent set of standards of behavior and expectations for their children. If this is just not possible, then at least one consistent parent is better than none. Children are usually quite intuitive. They know whether you care about them or not. If you do, there is no reason why you cannot say "no" to them when no is called for or expect them to do their homework or jobs around the house or be on time for family activities and behave in a generally respectable manner. Harshness is never called for. But if they anger you, get angry, and then make up. If you feel you are trying to do the right thing and they succeed in making you feel negligent or unfeeling, try not to overreact to this by being unduly permissive or indulgent on the one hand or punitive on the other.

There are, of course, ultimately, some decided advantages that can accrue to children because of the divorce. One of the most noteworthy is the opportunity for them to have two parents, both of whom can truly feel free to be themselves. For when parents have been entangled in an unhealthy kind of equilibrium, it is all too common for them, in their attempts to keep the marriage going, to forfeit a good deal of their own character. One man, having taken a compliant and somewhat subdued position in his relationship with his former wife to avoid repeated conflicts or crises that could never be settled, was seen by his three children as a rather shadowy figure, while their mother seemed the strong one in the family. The divorce brought a dramatic change in this pattern. Once on his own, this man could now define for himself the kind of person he wanted to become and the sort of life he wanted to lead. He renewed interests that had been abandoned during his marriage. He learned to be more outspoken about his convictions and more independent in his thinking, thus giving his children a more distinct father image with whom to relate and becoming someone for whom they could have more respect.

While divorce brings with it changes that children must confront, second marriages compound the possible problems. It is important for you to realize that the children of your partner as well as your own may still be suffering adverse reactions from the former marriage as well as from the impact of the divorce itself. It may have taken them some time to adapt to a new set of living conditions with divorced parents, and you are now about to impose still another on them. It will not be easy, even though what you imagine and intend to offer is the security of a new family structure.

If you want to know how children feel when their parents marry again—and how they do feel varies enormously—just ask them. A fourteen-year-old girl put it this way: "I was eight when my parents were divorced. My mother never remarried. I missed my father a lot in the beginning, but finally I began to believe him when he said he would always be around to see me and my sister, and I felt better. Dad spent a lot of time with us, taking us to do something nearly every weekend. We spent a month with him in the summer.

"He had lots of girl friends. They were mostly nice to us, but I knew that Dad wasn't taking any of them too seriously. Then, when his new wife came into the picture, I could tell it was going to be different. They'd hold hands a lot and kiss and she'd spend the weekend with us in the apartment, even though they didn't sleep in the same bedroom. When Dad told me he was going to marry her, I got scared. I liked her, but I was afraid I wouldn't see him any more. Mom didn't help the matter any when she kept saying that Dad would have a *new* family now.

"When I finally got up the guts to ask him, 'Will you still see us after you marry?' he told me things wouldn't change. But they did. Instead of spending a whole weekend, we'd go down to his place on Saturday afternoon, stay for dinner, and go home that night. My stepmother had two children of her own, and there wasn't any room for us to stay overnight. I used to have a small china decoration on the door of my room with my name on it. Dad left it there, but it didn't mean anything. It wasn't my room anymore."

For many children, remarriage involves another loss, the end of their life with a single parent. Their reactions can be quite complex. They may feel a need to put some distance between themselves and the new partner of their mother or father, out of loyalty to the other parent. They may feel downright resentful at what they experience as an intrusion into the closeness that they have—or feel they have—with the parent who has married again. Their radar is alert for the smallest sign of rejection. And again, these reactions are far more common among children who are old enough to appreciate what is happening and yet too young to have established their own lives.

Liz and Arthur Endicott illustrate the complexities of trying to combine two families after remarriage. At the time of their marriage, Liz's two little girls, Cindy and Amanda, were six and eight years old respectively. They had maintained a loving and close relationship with their father, Sam. Arthur had three children—a boy, Mark, fourteen; a daughter, Melissa, twelve; and a younger son, David, who was ten. Liz's children liked Arthur. They called him Uncle Arthur. Arthur liked them, although he sometimes felt uneasy about the fact that he could not really feel quite the same toward the girls as he did toward his own children. It was Liz, in fact, who reassured him that this was unrealistic. "I wouldn't expect you to," she said, "nor should you expect me to have the same feelings about yours that I do toward my own. I like them. In some ways I love them. But they can never be the same as my own."

Arthur's children, however, were somewhat more of a problem. Like Liz, he had been divorced for three years. His eldest child was eleven at the time of the divorce, and Arthur had spent many happy weekends taking his children to the country, swimming, eating pizza and Big Macs, and generally doing all the things that a single father does with children who do not live with him. They had become quite close, a sort of self-sufficient family unit unto themselves. At the same time, they had a separate life with their mother, who was quite diligent in her care for them and who, most of the time, tried consciously not to confront them with her resentment toward their father.

When their mother, Sarah, learned of Arthur's intention to marry again, however, this resentment was intensified. She bluntly told the children that now that their father was marrying again they should not expect the same degree of love and attention from him that they had grown used to in the past. "He'll have a new family now," she warned ominously. Arthur's son, Mark, now fourteen, acted unconcerned, but twelve-year-old Melissa and ten-year-old David were quite apprehensive. They were especially wary about Liz and kept their eyes open for any signs of indifference or rejection from her. Arthur shared this concern, although Liz went out of her way to make the children feel welcome by planning picnics, preparing large Sunday dinners, talking about all the children, hers and Arthur's, as if they were part of one big family. Even so, one of the worst arguments that she and Arthur had during the first year of their marriage was about the children. Sarah had implied in a telephone conversation with Arthur that their daughter, Melissa, had complained about "not feeling at home" with him any more. Arthur was upset. He told Liz about the remark, tentatively, as if he half believed it. Liz's feelings were deeply hurt and after the initial pain she became furious: "I've spent hours preparing meals and making plans for things for us all to do together and you pick up on a comment that your former wife makes which may or may not be true, and now you wonder if there is some basis to it." After she calmed down, Liz and Arthur were able to sort out the pieces and realize that their sensitivity to making the children feel comfortable in the structure of their new marriage had also made them especially vulnerable to Sarah's attitudes.

Such sensitivity is common, since most men and women marrying again are concerned about the impact of remarriage on their children and are keenly motivated to try to understand and be friendly with each other's children. They are also sharply aware of even the slightest evidence of trouble between one of their own children and the stepmother or stepfather, and when they think that a situation of dislike or rejection exists, they experience the painful dilemma of divided loyalty. In most instances, this concern is exaggerated or without any basis at all. It is difficult enough for parents to accept the ordinary disagreements that they will encounter with their own children—the sulking, the back-talk, the episodes of defiance, the need for discipline. How much more difficult it is when the children are "his" or "hers."

After they had been married a year, Liz and Arthur ran into real difficulties with his son, Mark. It began when the boy stopped coming with the others to visit them on weekends. Somehow, at the last minute, Sarah would call and say that Melissa and David were coming but Mark had something else to do. Arthur suspected that Sarah might be covering up for the boy's unwillingness to come although it would be out of character for Sarah not to take advantage of such an opportunity to make him feel uncomfortable. But she was not. When Arthur confronted his son with the question of why, in three months, he hadn't come over to the house once, the boy simply replied, "Because I don't want to" and offered no further explanation.

"Don't put the blame on me," Liz exclaimed when Arthur related the conversation to her. "I've tried my best." Arthur knew she had and began to wonder what he had done wrong. In a few months he saw more clearly what the problem really was: adolescence.

To begin with, Mark really preferred to be with his friends. Gone were the days when Arthur could pack the three children into the back of his station wagon and they could go off to the lake for the weekend. Secondly, the boy was engaged in the usual teenage process of testing limits. He was trying to find out how much he might be able to get away with. And precisely because Arthur and his mother were so often at odds with each other, he discovered that there was no firm and united front to push against. Instead, there was only the vacuum created by Arthur's anxiety and his mother's bewilderment, and consequently he went well beyond reasonable limits in his behavior.

He stayed out until three or four in the morning on weekends and refused to tell his mother where he had been. He failed to complete several papers for class and was nearly expelled from the private school that he attended because of his negative attitude toward work and his occasional, but noticeable, absences. It was only because of his previously good record and the fact that he had always been a very likable and considerate young man, bright and talented in many ways, that the headmaster gave him another chance.

Sarah began making frantic calls to Arthur. "The boy's room is a mess. He won't do anything I tell him. He'll have to go live with you. I can't take much more of this." Ironically, though predictably enough, her desperation brought the parents together for the first time in years and Arthur actually found himself telling Mark that he had to treat his mother with respect. Arthur, Sarah, and Mark went out to dinner one evening together to talk things out. The boy cried as he spoke about being lonely and not knowing what he wanted to do with himself. At other moments he would show flashes of anger toward his parents and ask them, "Just what do you expect of me?" Arthur set up a list of reasonable rules for Mark to live by: telling his mother where he was and when he intended to come home, for example, and taking the time to clean up his room and meeting the ordinary academic demands his teachers placed on him. The next few months proved that their attempt to meet Mark's rebelliousness coherently and together had paid off. Mark started coming by his father's house about once a month for dinner. He actually liked Liz, although he had not given himself much of a chance to get to know her. On Liz's birthday the boy sent her a present, a scarf which he had saved his allowance to buy and which was intended to tell her he cared.

Liz and Arthur encountered another problem common to families that have been intertwined through a second marriage. They each held somewhat disparate views about raising children. Liz was more of a disciplinarian and believed in strictness; Arthur was inclined to be more lenient. Liz felt children should be pressured to achieve. Arthur felt that they should not. He did not interfere when he thought that she was too harsh in punishing her own children, although he would sometimes cringe mentally. She would criticize him from time to time when it seemed to her that he was spoiling his own children and this would irritate him. "For a long time we had a home with two standards of behavior, in a way. But gradually she became less rigid in her approach to the girls and I became firmer with my kids, especially after the experience with young Mark."

Another risk to the parents of children in a second marriage is competitiveness. Like it or not, some youngsters are brighter than others, some are better-looking, some are more socially adept, some have serious emotional or physical problems. Be careful not to feel too fortunate, or unfortunate, as the case may be, comparing your children with those of your new partner. Liz had a competitive streak in her. From time to time she would upset Arthur by comparing the excellent school performances of her two little girls with the less conspicuously impressive record of his son, Mark, and his daughter, Melissa. She rarely made any reference to David's excellent performance.

"My girls are Harvard material," she would say, half teasing, half serious. "I think that Mark and Melissa would do well at some little college in the country somewhere, in New Jersey maybe." This led to more than one dispute until she learned to curb her urge to compete in the wrong arena.

The problems that Liz and Arthur faced are typical of those which people entering second marriages with children have to expect. It takes time and considerable effort to integrate so many different personalities of all ages into a new and more complex family unit. Each child has his and her own needs and preferences, likes and dislikes, and these include other children. Even as some brothers and sisters get along well and others squabble with each other on principle, so too will stepbrothers and stepsisters form a wide variety of relationships that range from mutual disdain to marrying each other a dozen years later. Newly remarried, you must expect such disparities and should attempt to achieve as much mutual respect for each other as you can. Treating all the children fairly does not mean equally, for their needs will vary from time to time and age to age. It does mean acknowledging the fact that they are all deserving of love and attention, without ignoring the inevitable truth that we usually feel more deeply about our own.

As a rule, you can assume the person you have married is well intentioned, trying his or her best to do the right thing. However, this is not always the case. Horror stories do exist, have always existed, and will most likely continue to do so. Seduction is one ugly example of a number of dramatic and damaging situations that can arise between stepparents and stepchildren. A twenty-three-year-old girl consulted a psychiatrist because she was extremely depressed and had made an abortive attempt to commit suicide. Her doctor discovered that she had been fourteen when her widowed mother had remarried. She was an only child. When she was sixteen, her stepfather came to her room one night while her mother was away visiting her grandmother. He sat on the edge of her bed and began to caress her intimately. She was quickly aroused. It was not her first sexual encounter, and she had had sexual fantasies involving her stepfather for over a year. They completed the sexual experience. From then on, whenever the mother was away, she and her stepfather had sexual relations until she was twenty. She experienced some guilt about her behavior, feeling that she was betraying her mother, but until she left for college went on with the affair, blocking out its real emotional impact. After the relationship ended she developed strong hostility toward her stepfather which she subsequently directed toward any man with whom she became emotionally or sexually involved.

Money and property may become issues. A man of thirty was confronted with his widowed father's remarriage. He and his father had previously been quite close. His father, a successful businessman, had acquired a fortune worth more than a million dollars. When the father, now sixty-three, married again to a woman of fifty, he assured his son that he need not be concerned about financial matters. But one afternoon, while alone in his father's study, the son came across a legal document. It was a prenuptial agreement that left his father's entire estate to his new wife in the event of his death, totally excluding his son. He was stunned. "Why?" he thought. "How could my father do this to me? How can I bring it up to him?" The young man did finally confront him with his discovery. At first his father denied it. Then he explained that his new wife had insisted on it before she would marry him, asking why she should take care of him in his old age and then be left without sufficient funds if and when he died. The marriage eventually ended in divorce, which nullified the agreement, but the father's relationship with his son could never be restored to its previous level of confidence.

Subtle but effective attempts at alienation are another example. A girl of fourteen who had been close to her father since her mother's departure—an abrupt but permanent desertion—several years earlier welcomed his intention to marry again to a woman his own age with four children of her own. Gradually, over a period of five years, her stepmother embarked on a subtle but incredibly successful campaign to alienate the father from his own daughter. The girl was sent to boarding school.

The stepmother often made allusions to the girl's so-called "sexual looseness" and whenever she would write to her father for allowance, the stepmother would subtly infer that the young girl was "greedy." When she came home for visits she was treated like a Cinderella. She was expected to do the chores around the house, while her stepbrothers and sisters were free to do whatever they wanted. She slept in the guest room. A woman clever at inducing guilt in others, this stepmother made the girl feel that, somehow, the discomfort and lack of welcome that she now experienced whenever she was home was her own doing and that she had not adjusted with generosity to her father's new life. Eventually, the girl simply stopped going home. Her father attributed this to her selfishness and no reconciliation ever occurred between them.

Children of people married a second time do not usually face such destructive situations. More often the new and complex set of interrelationships and the infusion of new people into the family can have quite a constructive impact, one that is stimulating to creativity and growth. From a new stepparent, for example, children may gain an appreciation of some subject, a new set of values, a new perspective on human relationships, that their own mother or father may not have provided. They may form relationships with stepbrothers and stepsisters that can endure throughout their lives.

Another circumstance deserves consideration: the birth of a child to the new couple. Three years after they married, when Liz was thirty-four and Arthur forty-three, they had another child, a little girl named Winnie. Arthur had been anxious about having another child. His youngest two had expressed concern to him about this possibility, and he felt a bit old. But Liz had always wanted a third child, and particularly one with Arthur.

Arthur's daughter, Melissa, took an immediate fondness for Winnie, volunteering to babysit whenever Arthur and Liz wanted to go anywhere. His son, David, and Liz's daughter, Cindy, were the godparents when the infant was christened. Slowly but surely, Winnie's presence began to be felt throughout the entire family system.

As Winnie grew, she was obviously a bright, affectionate, energetic child, with a keen sense of humor. Arthur felt a joy he had not known for years at the unambivalent greeting that Winnie gave him when he arrived home. "It's the only time in your life when anyone loves you without any qualifications," he often thought. Winnie certainly brought Arthur and Liz closer to each other.

Some years before, while still divorced, Arthur had stopped in a porcelain shop in Copenhagen. Standing on a shelf next to each other were three blue and white Bing and Grundahl figurines. They resembled his sons and daughter and he bought them to place on a bookshelf at home. After Winnie was born he began searching for a similar porcelain of her, going from one shop to another without any luck. It took him two years to find it, but finally he came upon a small, blond-haired, round-faced child with her hands raised up and reaching out, welcoming everyone to her. This was, without doubt, Winnie.

Winnie at three years of age had a lovely and special lack of self-consciousness, a "Hi there, I'm Winnie" kind of greeting, warm, sparkling, self-possessed. She had a good sense of humor, sometimes mimicking her stepsisters by half jokingly, half inadvertently calling her father "Uncle Arthur." She would sometimes spend time trying to figure out just what the relationships were among all the people in her world. Whenever Arthur was reminded of the turmoil that his divorce caused, with the lonely years between marriages and the problems created for his first three children, he would ask himself if it had all been worth it. He would inevitably think, "Out of all the sadness and trouble, Winnie was meant to be and all that was the price paid for her arrival." Winnie even thawed Sarah's heart. As Sarah grew to care about the child, her attitude toward Liz and Arthur improved even more.

For some couples in second marriages, the birth of another child can reinforce the cohesiveness of the marriage and restore a strong sense of family, as it did for Liz and Arthur. Until then, there may be a natural sense of dividedness—his family and hers. After that, the feeling of one family is often regenerated. The introduction of only one individual to a system of people can change the character of the entire system.

There are, of course, innumerable instances of people in second marriages who choose not to have more children. They feel they are too old. There are children enough. They are too independent. The choice of whether to have a child in a second marriage is a complex one, and an affirmative choice is best made after some of the waves that the new marriage has caused have settled down and both husband and wife feel that the marriage is going to work out well.

Cinderellas there are and wicked stepparents there will always be. But more often than not, stepparents give a good deal of themselves to their stepchildren. Psychiatrists have seen this often, a kind of heroism and generosity of spirit, when a stepmother or stepfather may befriend and support a youngster who has been the victim of some severe emotional disorder, such as schizophrenia. There are, in fact, innumerable situations in which stepparents shift the balance of an entire family to a better, more harmonious and healthy level, generating a home environment in which everyone, children and all, can grow strong.

14

The Family Connection

In a world that too often seems to foster anonymity and mutual indifference, we could all do with some people around us who care. Whether we call them family and friends or, as behavioral scientists would put it, social support systems, such people are critical to our well-being. We need them to confide in; we require their backing. They affect our ability to adapt to change and we, in turn, must learn new ways to relate to them as we move from marriage to being single again and then to another marriage.

Contemporary social conditions, such as industrialization, mobility, the high cost of owning homes large enough for extended families, have weakened family ties, making such support tenuous. Nor has psychological theory been an entirely positive influence, with Freud and a number of others pointing an accusing finger at parents, brothers, sisters as the cause of our repressions and anxieties. More recently, behavioral scientists have demonstrated how crucial family interactions are in determining whether we are to have a healthy outlook toward life or one that is self-destructive. R. D. Laing was a leader in popularizing the concept that family members position themselves in interlocking roles, usually at one person's expense. Someone is strong. Another is weak. Someone is the guiding light. Someone else is the martyr. One person is singled out as the loser or, more dramatically, as the sick one. Laing maintained that to be of any help to the person trapped in the sick position, a therapist would have to force a reshuffling among all the family members and that without a significant breaking down of roles, the patient could never succeed in abandoning his disability and be permitted, by the others, to assume a more self-assured stance in life.

The net result of all this has been to reinforce the idea that our families may simply not be good for us. Many people have become convinced that if they wish to maintain their freedom and the right to lead their own lives the less family they are involved with the better. Certainly there are times when this is true—when, for example, two thousand children die each year in this country as a result of child abuse.

However, it is not so simple to cut the ties. All of us, whether we like it or not, carry significant traces of our family's motivations, values, and premises within ourselves which we cannot so easily discard. Besides, why give up an important source of emotional support unnecessarily?

Recently, a Washington, D.C. psychiatrist has extended the limits of traditional psychotherapy in the way it explores with patients the influence their families have had on them. Instead of just talking about them, he advises patients to seek out as many living relatives as they can. Find out, he instructs them, as much as possible about the nature of your family. What was your grandmother really like? What kind of life did the family have before coming to this country? How well did your mother and dad communicate with each other? Why did they have only one child, you? The ultimate goal of this technique is not only the information acquired but a coming to terms with your family—solving areas of conflict and misunderstanding, if it can be done. It is better, according to this therapist, to achieve some degree of harmony together with your family than all alone in the confines of the consulting room. It is a form of counter-alienation.

Learning to relate to your family is never static. It becomes an ongoing endeavor as you move from one stage of your life to another. And when you enter a second marriage, you inevitably move into a whole new system of interpersonal relationships which has its own character. You are bringing with you your own set of relationships that will, somehow or other, blend or conflict with the system you are entering. Of course this happened before, when you married the first time, but now you will find you have some important advantages.

To begin with, your parents and other family members (except, of course, your children) are definitely not going to be as influential in affecting your choice of partner. You are older. You are freer. You have been through one marriage and have reestablished a life of your own. Pleasing them or rebelling against their wishes is not likely to play a significant part in your motivation.

Moreover, parents are usually much more realistic the second time. However concerned they may have been the first time—were you old enough, was the man or woman you were marrying good enough for you, was your prospective bride's or bridegroom's background up to your own—they now have far more reasonable expectations. The seventy-year-old father of a thirty-three-year-old remarried woman described this difference. "When my daughter married her former husband, I was very concerned about a lot of things I now look on as superficial. His parents were friends of ours. I knew she was unsure of herself at that time, but her mother and I pushed it. When we found out he started playing around when she was pregnant with their first child, we were shocked. This time we're letting her make up her own mind. The man she's marrying is fifteen years older than she is. We would have violently opposed that then. Not now. He's a decent sort. I suppose if he had some real problem, like drinking, we'd take a stand, but he doesn't. It's her life and we're old-fashioned enough to rather see her married than not." Her mother, on the other hand, while she had no specific objections, was vaguely uneasy, sensing that, since her prospective son-in-law was older and a more affirmative person, she would not have as much to say about her daughter's life as she had had in the past.

This brings up another important point—that in marrying again, neither you nor your new husband or wife are likely to assume a childlike position in relation to either parents or new in-laws. Hence you have a better chance of forming a healthier marital bond and of decreasing the possibility of your marriage being adversely affected by family patterns and pressures.

A more adult interaction shows up in little ways. The first time you married you may have called your new in-laws Mother and Dad. Or perhaps you weren't sure what to call them, so you avoided calling them anything until, after some years, they invited you to use their first names. You may even have gone on calling them Mr. and Mrs. Whoever. The second time around everyone rapidly moves onto a first-name basis, clearly symbolizing the equality that exists in the relationships.

The deeper implications of this contrast were well described by a forty-five-year-old remarried man. "The first time I married, my wife's parents definitely became my substitute parents. I see that clearly now. Actually, I knew it then. I had had a lot of problems with my own family. My father had a long history of business failures. My mother was chronically depressed. In comparison, my former wife's family looked pretty good. Then, too, I was pretty impressed with the size of her family. I had been an only child; she had two brothers and two sisters. I saw myself getting not just a wife but a whole new family." As the years progressed this man grew disenchanted with his foster family. He came to realize that his wife's brothers and sisters were engaged in a concealed but vicious and deadly competitiveness with each other. His new mother-in-law was a despot who ruled the home, while his father-in-law, in spite of his professional success and prominence, smoldered weakly in the shadows.

"I kept looking to them for approval. None came. One of the family's major patterns was that attention could only be had by getting into trouble. One sister-in-law was always center stage and stayed there by going through three husbands and two nervous breakdowns. Then there was something else. Even though my father-in-law was a very successful attorney, with everyone else there seemed to be an underlying contempt for achievement. Neither of my wife's brothers finished college. When I became vice-president of the company I was then working for, they totally ignored my promotion."

When this man, feeling more and more uneasy about his in-laws' influence on his own self-esteem as well as on his marriage, began to try to put some distance between himself and them, the result was increasing friction between himself and his wife. As long as he had unwittingly played the role of being another child in her parents' family, the marriage remained in equilibrium. But as soon as he started to break away, he discovered, to his dismay, where his wife's real loyalties were directed. "I can't live with someone who's going to treat my family this way" was one of his wife's last angry comments.

He married again at thirty-eight, to a divorced woman in her early thirties. This time "I wasn't looking for a family. I was looking for a wife. I'd grown to view my own parents' limitations a lot more realistically. In spite of the fact that he had not been that good handling money, Dad was a good father, always willing to spend time with me and hear me out. Sure, Mother had been depressed, but she was always kind and supportive."

His new wife's family was not without its problems. Her parents had divorced when she was sixteen, and they were still not on very good terms with each other. "My wife and I had a pretty good reading of the situation. We talked about it openly. We were both determined not to get drawn into the center of her parents' difficulties."

Arriving at a mutual understanding with your new husband or wife regarding how you will deal with each other's family is a critical part of making your new marriage work. You can never afford to underestimate the residual attachments that each of you have to your families even if you are far away from them both in miles and life experiences.

You may be fortunate. You may discover a high degree of compatibility with a new mother-in-law or father-in-law and so gain some valuable friends. It certainly makes life easier when this is the case.

Frequently, however, you may have very little in common with them, except that you have married one of their children. You will still spend time with them, and the question is how? The best course of action is to identify and develop any mutual interests to use as a point of contact. For example, a fifty-year-old writer married one of his editors who was twelve years younger than he. Her parents were pleasant people. Her mother had been a bookkeeper until her retirement; her father was a postal worker. They were duly impressed by the accomplishments of their new son-in-law, but beyond that there was little for all of them to talk about when they were together. However, they did enjoy playing cards. It was their favorite pastime. So their new son-in-law, who had had neither the time nor the inclination to play bridge or canasta since his time spent as a journalist in the Korean War, made up his mind to refresh his card skills, and their bimonthly rounds of bridge became something to which they all looked forward.

Coping with new in-laws is not always so simple. They may favor your new partner's previous husband or wife and show it, either openly or subtly. They may try to place the same demands on you as they did on a former son- or daughter-in-law, demands which you may well consider excessive, such as spending every weekend with them at a summer place or including them whenever you entertain friends. If the parental attachment between your new husband or wife is unusually strong, it is probably best for you to allow and in fact encourage your partner occasionally to spend time with them alone, without you, to both satisfy their needs as well as your partner's sense of obligation. Since you undoubtedly have your own set of responsibilities—parents of your own, children by a previous marriage, perhaps some special project—it should be possible for you to construct such a routine without making your in-laws feel you are intentionally rejecting them.

Some in-laws, however, are masters at manipulation

and guilt induction. They know how to make you feel rotten—and usually angry at the same time—when you do not do exactly what they want. But don't make the mistake of going to war with them. Open hostilities can severely strain your relationship with your new spouse. It is just as unwise, on the other hand, to bend over backward to accommodate their every wish. Such accommodation will only encourage further abuse, while you accumulate a considerable amount of repressed fury that might well get displaced onto your husband or wife rather than directed toward your in-laws themselves.

The answer to such sticky situations lies in being able to set limits and, most importantly, to do so with the collaboration of your partner. Sometimes such lines of demarcation are a matter of policy. You and your partner decide, beforehand, approximately how much time you will spend with the family and how that time will be spent, and you stick to this arrangement.

At other times limit-setting has to be done on the spot. "I was spending last weekend at my husband's family's house," one woman described. "His father is a tyrant. His mother is no better. My husband knows this, but he wants to keep peace, so he does a lot of giving in. Saturday afternoon I was in the kitchen and my father-in-law shouted from the other room, 'Bring me a glass of beer.' I felt my temper beginning to boil over. Instead I brought him the beer and suggested, politely but firmly, that next time he say 'please' rather than shouting an order at me. He looked startled. But it was the last time he addressed me in that way."

You must be careful, however, not to assume that because your new husband or wife seems quite independent of his or her family that the blood ties are not still rather strong. Arthur Endicott initially failed to appreciate the complex interaction between his new wife,

Liz, and her mother. Liz's mother had a knack for upsetting her. She was often critical, of the way Liz treated the children, how Liz kept her home, even how she treated Arthur. Not infrequently, after a phone conversation with her mother, Liz would feel exasperated and irritable and slightly depressed. At times she would vent her anger against her mother to Arthur, who, in turn, would become angry with Liz's mother for upsetting Liz and more or less as a matter of principle.

One evening, after Liz hung up the phone and grumbled something about her mother, Arthur, trying to be sympathetic, commented, rather automatically, "Look, it's clear that woman can really be a bitch." Liz spun around, livid, and suggested that he keep such comments about her mother—or anyone else in her family, for that matter—to himself, that he had no right to be critical of them, and that she could find a number of similar things to say about his family if she chose to.

In other words, be careful not to make hurtful or critical remarks about your new husband's or wife's family—abruptly stating an unpleasant insight you think might be useful—unless you are quite sure your mate is really open to some new understanding or is in a mood to share what might be seen as the humor of it. As a rule, an attack on one's family will be interpreted as an attack on oneself.

But even when you are discreet and tactful, there are other stresses that your new in-laws will contribute to your marriage which you should not underestimate. Because most people entering second marriages are somewhat older, their parents will be older, too. And so, without the background of years of sharing responsibilities, the new couple will often have to face the problems of parents' aging. One husband and wife had to arrange for the funeral of the husband's father within a week after their marriage, following a sudden and unexpected heart attack. Then, a month later, they had to arrange for her mother, who had been becoming progressively senile, to enter a nursing home.

It is important to expect such problems, especially the eventuality of death. The death of a significant family member, especially a parent, can seriously affect your marriage for a while. If its impact is not recognized, it can irreversibly damage your new life together. Your reaction to the death of your parent or even an in-law can be quite complex, with the impact of grief being delayed and showing up months or even a year or more after the death itself. Moreover, it can last longer than is acknowledged by those people who believe in pulling oneself together and going on with life. It is not hard to see how the effects of grief—a waning sexual interest, a sensitivity to rejection, a tendency to withdraw from interpersonal contacts, a chronic irritability and tension—can readily and erroneously be assumed to reflect some deterioration in the marital relationship, giving rise to unnecessary conflict and alienation.

As the ties that traditionally linked families together have grown weaker, friendships have come to play an even greater part in one's social support system. Who are our friends? Where do they come from? First, there are those you went to school with. Few of these friendships, some reduced to forced reminiscences at reunions, will survive unless you still happen to remain in the same community. When you marry the first time you are likely to sift through the friends you acquired at college and work; those who do not fit into your new life as a couple gradually disappear from the scene.

Although the pattern is changing somewhat as more and more women continue to work after marriage, in the lives of most married couples the wife is the one who determines the social life the couple will have. The reason for this seems to lie in the different patterns this society sets between the way women and men develop and cultivate friendships. In part the explanation is a psychological one: Men seem willing to consider themselves friends and act accordingly even when they have very little contact with each other. Women seem to want to spend more time on a continuing basis with the women they feel close to.

In part this is cultural, in part circumstantial. By and large, the men's club, the place for a drink on the way home or a round of backgammon in the evening is a thing of the past. There is little enough time for family life as it is. At work, the average man is surrounded by other men with whom he may form friendships but generally only superficial ones since, in the back of his mind, he thinks of their alternate roles as competitors. Never encouraged to be emotionally open, he tends to avoid sharing intimacies with the men he knows. In a way, with the husbands of his wife's friends, he feels curiously safe as long as they do not significantly outrank him in power or wealth.

In contrast, our society has traditionally allotted to women more frank and intimate relationships with each other, thereby strengthening the bond among them. And so, with such friendships being stronger and longer-lasting, women tend to keep old friends after marriage, with their husbands entering the circle. The husband's male friends, on the other hand, are more likely to marry away from this group and into circles created by their own wives. Even when the wife's friends' husbands are found less than interesting, they are usually tolerated by the husband because of the closeness that exists between the women. With this pattern established, new friends will start to come from the wife's life—meeting in the park over strollers, or her colleagues or clients, and these new couples, too, will become incorporated into the new social life.

If a marriage ends in the death of one partner, the widow or widower seldom experiences any loss of friendships. Quite the contrary. Nearly everyone rallies to their aid. However the picture is quite different in the case of divorce. Because of the nature of the social structure—its marked involvement with the wife and the wife's friends—the divorced woman usually finds herself with a good deal of support, while her ex-husband initially finds himself with little or none. A few of her friends may feel slightly threatened by her presence if their husbands find her appealing, but this is ordinarily not a significant problem. Her main concern may eventually be to find some men whose company she enjoys, but her former husband's main concern for some while may be just finding anyone he can count on or talk to.

By the time you meet, you and your future partner will have each developed a new set of friends. Many of them are especially suited to your single life. Some are dedicated to being bachelors, male or female. Many have been divorced themselves. With some you may have been involved in a sexually and emotionally intimate way, for a while at least. Remarriage brings about another reshuffling, not unlike the one that took place when you married the first time. With a few notable exceptions, the friends who are married are more easily integrated into your new life than those who are not. If you or your new husband or wife especially dislike some former friend, you may have to continue the relationship separately or drop it altogether. In creating your new social life, there are some guidelines that will help you do so more smoothly.

It is best for you and your new partner to intentionally

set out to meet new people for the purpose of creating a set of social relationships that are truly suited to the two of you as a couple. Friends from the past who fit in well are fine, but it is also important to cultivate new friendships together.

Both of you should be motivated and encouraged to sustain old friendships with people of the same sex and to include them and their partners into your life if feasible.

Select your friends with care. Never underestimate the influence they can have on the course of your marriage. Envy and competitiveness can be strong drives, and in the guise of being helpful, many a so-called friend has taken a problem which a couple has been trying to deal with and turned it into a major conflagration.

Fortunately, nowadays, you will not have to be concerned about the social repercussions that remarried couples once had to face. You will not have to quit beach clubs or move to new neighborhoods or change jobs because people around you disapprove of your conduct. But you will have to learn how to overcome some degree of self-consciousness when you run into people who were (and still may be) friends of your former husband or wife and who once seemed to be your friends as well. Only civility and courtesy are called for.

Finally, we come to a particularly knotty problem. If you have been single for a while, you may have had a number of sexual affairs that are now over. In the interests of your new marriage, you should take a cold, hard look at these. While a few exceptional friendships of this type may be carried over, most will have to be dropped. If you have had a very intense love relationship with someone in the past, it is unrealistic to expect to remain close friends after you marry again, especially if your new husband or wife is aware of the details. (They are likely to be, and you are probably the one who told them.) The ongoing presence of such a person in your new life can be threatening. It can delay the formation of mutual trust and easily stir up jealousy. There may be scenes, arguments, with you defending the innocence of the relationship as it now stands, while your partner thinks of seeking out some old flame to show you just what it feels like. Offended, you may even be tempted to renew the affair out of hurt pride. Such old, close relationships from your single years can really endure only when the intimate aspects have been over for some time, when both you and a former lover possess genuine respect for the importance and integrity of your new marriage, and, most importantly, when it is acceptable to your new husband or wife. For regardless of how sexually free you may have been in the past, a second marriage, to last, requires fidelity even more than a first.

15

The Case for Fidelity

With the current emphasis on self-fulfillment and liberation, many of us have decided that, with only one life to live, we should be able to enjoy as many of life's pleasures as possible. Sexual pleasure rates high on the scale of gratifying experiences. Moreover, many of us are convinced that a good sex life is essential to mental and physical health. In fact, the pursuit of an active sex life seems to have acquired the status of an inalienable right.

The national preoccupation with sex is not difficult to document. Just stroll past a newsstand, browse through any bookstore, or glance at the billboards outside a movie house. Erotica seems to have outshadowed all other concerns, except perhaps making money. Sex-therapy clinics have sprung up all over the country, some with long waiting lists. Many middle-aged people, raised in more conservative times, have come to envy the apparent freedom with which younger men and women engage in premarital sex. They conclude, however naïvely, that most of the problems they have had in their marriages could have been avoided if they, too, had had such freedom when they were young.

The women's liberation movement has given added impetus to the changing sexual mores. For one thing, it has spotlighted the hypocritical double standard, giving men that special license to sexual freedom, with women expected just to forgive, forget, and endure. Moreover, women are making it clear that they are just as entitled to sexual fulfillment as men, and, like many men, this desire is often expressed as a demand. "We have a real problem in our marriage," one thirty-four-year-old woman confided to her doctor. "My husband is in the mood to make love only about once a week, but that's nowhere near enough to satisfy me. I've read that I'm close to the prime of life when a woman's desires are at their height. But the more I talk to my husband about this situation, the more he backs away. What am I supposed to do now?"

The gradual liberalization of sexual standards for the unmarried of both sexes has received backing from the growing number of the formerly married. As one thirty-eight-year-old divorced woman stated: "If my husband and I had slept together when we were engaged, we would never have married. It was disastrous. I've told my children they should find out how good their sexual adjustment is with anyone they are thinking of marrying." Disappointed, disillusioned, often feeling cheated by life, many such men and women attribute their marital failures to sexual incompatibility. Once single again, they set out to find the perfect sexual involvement.

One result of the insistence on sexual fulfillment is that, in the minds of many, it has begun to take precedence over the ideal of fidelity in marriage. The concept of open marriage—where couples not only pursue separate interests but also have the option to seek outside sexual liaisons—has won a number of adherents. Even some psychiatrists, psychologists, and social scientists have suggested that occasional lapses from the rule of fidelity are in fact good for married couples. As one psychiatrist put it, "An outside love relationship often corresponds in time to a period of crisis in the marriage. One or the other feels blocked in personal growth, suffocated. The couple has not been able to work through some long-standing conflict. Through an affair, the one involved may gain some valuable new perspective into himself or herself and a new way of looking at marriage. A change for the better occurs. And although I never recommend revealing infidelities because, unlike some of my colleagues, I think it is harder to forgive and forget, if the affair is somehow discovered and the couple can resolve the hurt and sense of betrayal, a more mature and solid kind of bond can then be established."

Times have changed from the days when adulteresses were stoned in the public square or, in somewhat more civilized times, were not received in the better homes in town. The private detective who once earned a hundred dollars a day plus expenses using his camera and tape recorder to gather evidence for someone in search of a divorce has been forced by liberalized laws to turn his talents elsewhere. Whereas, only twenty years ago actress Ingrid Bergman's American film career was extinguished when it was revealed that she was involved in an extramarital affair, today, such news would scarcely cause a ripple of attention.

Should we all be persuaded, then, that for both sexes infidelity is neither unusual or wrong?

"Yes" would be a dangerous assumption for anyone entering a second marriage to make. For while it is true that people are less disapproving of infidelity in recent years and less punitive toward those involved, the affairs to which we react with compassion or mellow indulgence are usually someone else's affairs, not our own. It is one thing to overlook or be indifferent to the sexual indiscretions of film stars or casual aquaintances. It is quite another to be confronted with infidelity at home. There it is quite a different story.

"My husband and I had a perfectly good sexual relationship in the early years of our marriage. He's a good man. He never did anything to warrant what I did. In the eighth year of our marriage, just after our youngest son was born, I began this affair with my pediatrician. He told me he was unhappily married but had no intention of getting a divorce. That was all right because neither did I. At first it was ecstatic. I discovered a kind of sexual intimacy I had never known." The woman in therapy was now in her early fifties. "It continued in secrecy for nearly ten years. As time went on, I became more and more afraid of being caught. And I felt guilty. I had trouble sleeping. I'd get depressed and even think it might be better to die. But I couldn't break it off. I didn't want to.

"Finally, I told my husband about it. Like a confession. I didn't know how he'd react, but I felt I had to be honest. He was deeply hurt. He didn't show it, because he rarely shows his emotions openly. 'I can forgive you,' he said, 'but only if this never happens again.'

"That was ten years ago. The distance between us since has been unbearable. We're polite. We go on vacations together. We entertain. We talk about the children. We even make plans for his retirement. But he never touches me with real affection. If I ask him, he tells me he loves me, but that's all there is. I feel empty, vulnerable. If I had a chance to find someone else now, I would. But I'm not the type who believes in being unfaithful, you've got to understand that. It's just that I'm so miserable."

Her husband's version was simple, dispassionate. "I don't believe in divorce. I never was involved with anyone other than my wife. When she told me what had been going on, I wasn't surprised. I had a pretty good idea already. I thought of breaking our marriage up. But, for a lot of reasons, I decided not to. Do I love her? Certainly. And I forgive her. But I could never trust her again or want to be intimate with her. We do have sex, but it is more perfunctory, a matter of marital obligation now than anything else."

Infidelity, rather than being enriching, obliterates any real closeness between the couple. Even if it does not lead to the end of marriage, it often results in the kind of remoteness and quiet desperation that the above couple described. Open marriage in the sense of sexual freedom undoubtedly works best for those husbands and wives who really do not care too much for each other, or where the nature of their personalities is such that both are equally incapable of making a permanent commitment to anyone. They can enjoy the structure of marriage without its intimacy or responsibilities. Most of us, though, find it difficult to throw off casually the basic concept of marital fidelity which, having lasted over the centuries, can hardly disappear without a trace in a few decades.

Even though divorced men and women are strong advocates of sexual freedom, once they remarry they clearly revert to the rule of fidelity. They intend to remain faithful and expect the same of their new partners. Only under the most unusual and exceptional circumstances does a man or woman enter a second marriage with either a prenuptial understanding or a secret intent to pursue outside love relationships at will. There is, of course, always the rare exception, such as one man who was shocked to discover that his third wife had married him, when they were both in their mid-forties, for the explicit purpose of concealing the existence of an affair she had been having with another married man and which she fully intended to continue.

For the most part, people entering second marriages are keenly aware of how easily infidelity can destroy the formation of the new union and its chances for survival. Many of them have witnessed, first hand, the impact of infidelity on their own marriages. Having been through one divorce, they can more easily contemplate another, and, in spite of the pain or humiliation that may be associated with such an option, given the choice between living with someone who is unfaithful and ending the marriage, they are likely to do the latter.

While the moral condemnation of infidelity has declined, most people still regard it in a strongly negative way. Today perhaps the biggest change is in the language used for discussing adultery. No longer the language of good and evil, it has become instead the language of psychology. Extramarital affairs are viewed as symptoms of problems in the relationship between a husband and wife. But the new ground rules, based on valuing honesty in marriage, tell us that if your relationship with your husband or wife is so bad that you have to seek someone else outside the marriage, you should either straighten things out or take steps to extricate yourself from the marriage.

Realizing the risks, then, why do men and women in second marriages still become involved in extramarital relationships? We can find some clues in the Kinsey Report, many of the findings of which are no less relevant today than they were when compiled thirty years ago.

Kinsey found the following sexual patterns: Men who had active sexual lives before marriage were more inclined toward infidelity early on in marriage than those who did not; religion was a major deterrent to infidelity, especially among women; the peak for infidelity among women occurred during their mid- and late thirties and among men in their late forties and early fifties.

Since religion is not as strong a force in the lives of many Americans at the moment, despite some definite evidence of a reversal in this trend, and since both men and women who are involved in second marriages are closer to the critical ages for infidelity, they are probably more vulnerable to extramarital affairs when the proper motivation mix is present.

What are these motivations? Here are some of the more common ones:

1. Sexual incompatibility, real or presumed. A thirty-five-year-old woman, in desperation, sought out a lover because her husband not only became impotent but was unwilling to do anything to correct his lack of sexual desire or capacity. A forty-two-year-old man, married a second time, resumed a sexual relationship with a former lover because "My new wife didn't show enough interest in me as a person. She seemed to enjoy being my wife, being married, the social structure of it, but within months after we settled in together, she began to find every excuse to avoid going to bed with me."

2. A reaction to feeling rejected by your husband or wife. One woman, for example, engaged in a brief affair in her late twenties shortly after the birth of her third child because her husband had failed to visit her in the hospital. A man whose wife paid an extended trip to her parents' lavish summer home and left her husband working in a hot city had an affair with his secretary.

3. Coping with the traditional mid-life crisis. Approaching forty for women and fifty for men are critical points in life, ones that are often associated with feelings of depression and very deep concerns about aging and whether you will remain sexually attractive. A fifty-one-year-old businessman who had been faithful to his wife throughout their marriage seemed to go through an abrupt and drastic change in personality. Instead of dressing conservatively, as he usually did, he chose loud and wildly patterned shirts and suits. He neglected his responsibilities. At home he accused his wife of being dominating and controlling, neither of which remotely applied, and they began to have frequent arguments. He launched an affair with a woman in her thirties whom he had met at a company picnic. Completely different from his wife, less educated, less interesting, less attractive as a person, this woman had little in common with him other than an interest in passionate and uninhibited sex. As he grew increasingly dependent on her, he would spend more and more time in her apartment in the evenings. At home, he drank heavily and was morose and sullen. His wife, knowing what was going on, tried to persuade him to "come to his senses." Only when she seriously threatened legal separation did he try to end the affair and seek professional help. In treatment the man discovered that, not having been sexually active when he was young, he had missed going through the usual adolescent rebelliousness. And while he had been compliant and responsible as a teenager, now, at fifty, it was as if the undercurrents of adolescence were emerging at full force, at a time and in such a way that the damage to his life was extensive.

4. Unconscious, and sometimes not so unconscious, hostility. A thirty-four-year-old woman, married with

two children, had grown increasingly resentful over what she correctly perceived as her husband's selfishness and lack of consideration. She began an affair with a neighbor in the suburb where they lived and made no effort to keep it secret. Angry as he was, her husband was more willing to accept the embarrassment she caused him than to release his hold on his wife or be separated from his children.

Unconscious hostility operates somewhat differently because you are not really in touch with it. It often shows up as a sense of futility. In your marriage, it may appear as a loss of sexual desire, an urge to put distance between you and your partner. You may feel lonely. Unable to recognize or deal with your anger in a direct way, you are vulnerable to whatever opportunities come along for an extramarital sexual involvement. However fulfilling it may be, its origin and primary purpose is to express indirectly an anger that you cannot express directly toward your mate.

5. Lack of communication. People involved in extramarital relationships are likely to have marriages in which neither can communicate clearly and directly with each other, especially about topics that are emotionally charged or controversial. These are simply pushed aside in the interests of a superficial harmony. If you are unable to be direct, the reason may simply be a fear of disagreeable scenes. But there can also be a fundamental personality clash. You may be one type of person—sensitive, in touch with your emotions, intuitive—while your partner may be a pragmatic, down-to-earth, no-nonsense type of person who comes across as cold and dispassionate. When no bridge between such a polarity can be built, you will end up with an emotional vacuum into which infidelity can readily move.

6. The persistence of complex sexual problems. One young man of twenty-nine had a long history of visiting prostitutes several times a week. The urge to do so would come on him out of the blue or one of the prostitutes would call him, inviting him to meet her on his lunch hour. He married a woman with whom he had a good deal in common and with whom he had a good sexual relationship. They proceeded to have children. Nonetheless, he continued this pattern of extramarital activity, excusing himself on the basis of being "oversexed." In fact, he had serious doubts about his masculinity verging on a fear of being homosexual. The compulsive drive to keep reassuring himself of his potency and heterosexuality was not abated by marriage. When he developed venereal disease and had to reveal this to his wife, she insisted that he seek professional help. She was not threatened by fear of another woman but felt very insecure in the face of the "uncontrollable" nature of his behavior.

7. An inability to commit oneself to the marriage bond because of some inner personality difficulties. Here we find those people who are terrified of closeness and so must always keep one foot out the door in any relationship. There are those who are so dominant and competitive that they turn to extramarital affairs as a way to exert their dominance and independence, in a kind of one-upsmanship. There are also those who are so narcissistic, selfish, and self-absorbed that they do not even feel the need to be faithful, since they do not really value the relationship at all except for what they themselves get out of it. As a rule these people are skilled at introducing an on-again, off-again quality to any love relationship. They often have a unique ability to manipulate others, usually through sex. The mixed messages that they deliver are "I love you, but I really don't love you, I love myself

more, but—don't go away because I need you." Should you find yourself emotionally involved with such a person, you will have difficulty breaking away, since, as the behaviorists have shown, the psychological impact of mixed-message behavior is such that your need for, and dependency on, that person is increased.

Knowing the causes of infidelity will help you reconsider the current opinion that fidelity is a quaint vestige of past values and that it is not really relevant to marriage. In fact, infidelity almost always reveals that there is an instability in the marriage or something wrong within one or both of the individuals who are married.

Men and women entering second marriages must be particularly conscious of this fact. They do not have the external supports—children, family, a long history of having been married and weathering a variety of rough periods in life together—that are so critical in helping people in first marriages survive the impact of infidelity. It is the strength of the commitment and the interpersonal bond that make a second marriage work. This takes time to develop and it requires trust. The stresses that will act on it are potentially quite severe. Infidelity can destroy it.

The risk of discovery is not the only risk you run. There is also the risk of the effect that an outside entanglement can have on you as a person. You may find yourself in a state of conflict, not knowing whether to care more for your lover or for the person you are married to. You may have to become skilled at the art of deception, having to explain why you were not at home or in the office in the afternoon, or what movie you saw when you really didn't go to a movie at all. Moreover, there is only so far you can travel with the affair. Sooner or later you will have to figure out how to end it and bear with its ending. In addition, affairs take time, and for the remarried, faced with an incredible number of demands on their time, there is hardly enough time as it is.

But before an affair becomes a probability, there are certain guidelines you can follow to reduce the likelihood of injuring your second marriage by infidelity.

First, of course, you should choose wisely. Be sure that you and the person you are marrying are emotionally stable and capable of understanding what the commitment to marriage means.

Deal with each other in an open and honest manner. As conflicts arise, try to resolve them. Create an atmosphere in your relationship that permits each of you to express your feelings freely. Be resilient enough to be able to recover from moments of conflict, forgive, and go on.

You would probably not marry a second time without some assurance that your sexual relationship with your prospective partner was pretty good. Perhaps it is the best sexual involvement you have known. But if it is not, accept the fact that it is good enough.

Fidelity is an inherent part of the kind of psychological commitment that marriage requires. It has practical consequences as well. It forces you to work problems through instead of running away from them. And it reduces the likelihood of stirring up one of human nature's most destructive passions: jealousy. The standard of fidelity in marriage has been around since the dawn of history, and even if we cannot specify how or where it began, it has become part of those elements in mankind's collective unconscious designed to insure both individual and group survival.

You do have a decided edge in staying faithful the second time around. Unless you were married the first time at a very young age, and then only briefly, you have probably already been through and learned how to cope with the kind of problems that set people in first marriages up for extramarital encounters. Thrill-seeking is one example. The crisis of middle age is another. You don't have to give it "one more try." You already have. You have already faced the futility and turmoil that accompanied the end of your previous marriage and so, if you have been smart about it, you have learned better ways to deal with dissension, boredom, disillusionment, and all the other unpleasant situations that can lead to infidelity than to risk losing your new marriage.

You are more experienced and knowledgeable sexually. You are also more realistic, knowing that the original ardor and excitement, however great, cannot last indefinitely and that its mellowing should not be misinterpreted as a waning in love. You also know that you have to work creatively to keep sexual intimacy fresh and alive. As vital as sex is to a good marriage, you will not be likely to marry for sex as such. Moreover, you should be in a better position to keep sex in proper perspective as part of a large picture that emphasizes the quality of the human interaction between you and your new partner. For certainly this interaction, of which sex is only a part, is what will define your marriage.

16

First Aid for Second Marriages

People feel they have to be in desparate straits before they will seek out a therapist. They won't take this step unless they are extremely demoralized and feeling barely able to function. It is too bad that we can't learn to act sooner, but perhaps this is why emotional pain exists, to force us to do something so that it will go away. And of course the best way to do this is to correct the problems that have given rise to the pain in the first place.

However, as the idea of professional help has become more acceptable, more and more people involved in second marriages are consulting psychiatrists and other professionals for marital counseling. What reasons do they commonly give for seeking consultation? A sense of defeat is a prominent one. "I've tried for four years to make this marriage work," said one forty-eight-year-old woman, crying as she spoke. "I just feel hopeless about it. We seem to be pulling against each other all the time. My husband resents my career. He acts as though he's still married to his former wife half the time. We argue constantly over the amount of time he spends with his children and I can't stand his harshness with my three. We're both aware of the problem, but in spite of talking about it over and over again, nothing seems to change. What I want to know is should we go on or call it off?"

A sense of responsibility and guilt is another key motivation for seeking help. One young woman, Anne Brighton, thirty-three, had decided that her marriage of four months to forty-three-year-old David Brighton had been a mistake from the beginning. Still looking attractive despite her exhaustion, she sat down in the psychiatrist's office on the edge of the least comfortable chair, obviously ill-at-ease, afraid of being dissuaded from her decision to get a divorce. She quickly explained that she had come only because David had insisted on it. "He thinks there's something wrong with me because I don't want to go on with the marriage. He thinks I'm sick or something. I'm not. But I'm a fair person. I don't want to ruin his life, or my own for that matter. If there's any chance of it working out, I guess I owe it to both of us to try."

Sometimes there is a more dramatic catalyst—profound depression or a very specific and well-defined problem in the context of an otherwise good relationship. A sixty-two-year-old man, for example, consulted a psychiatrist a few times because, after ten years of marriage to a woman twelve years his junior, he had begun to have trouble with sex. "I can't sustain an erection as well as I used to, and sometimes I come prematurely. My wife is very patient with this. But it makes me worried. Is it just getting older? Do I have some hidden hostility toward her? I don't see how I could." His concern and his sexual problem subsided quickly when it became clear, through their discussions, that he was reacting to a period of stress in business and that his difficulties had no deeper roots.

On the whole those who turn to a professional for help with a second marriage are usually the same people who have sought guidance before rather than muddling through complex situations on their own. That is, at some time or other in their lives they have consulted a professional for another reason and, having found it of value, do so again. The level of education and general knowledge is relevant, since people with broader experience are more likely to consider the possible benefits than those who, in a categorical rejection of such help, assume that psychiatry and other such professionals are only for the mentally ill. "They never help anyone anyway. My sister has been seeing a therapist for fifteen years and she's not any better. Besides, they have a record of breaking up more marriages than they cure" are common misconceptions based on limited exposure but highly effective as deterrents to many who could well use some guidance.

Another major resistance is based on the inherent compulsion many feel to solve their problems themselves. We would never think of going into court without a lawyer or engaging in an Internal Revenue Service audit without a good accountant or performing a surgical operation on ourselves. But when it comes to personal problems, including marital relationships, pride enters the picture and the thought of professional help—with its time, effort, and cost—strikes many as being not only superfluous but humiliating. The mere decision to reach out for guidance seems an admission of hopelessness and helplessness. Not only does it make many feel that their marriages are finished, but it may seem somehow to introduce a dampening element that threatens to rob relationships of what little intimacy and romance remain in them.

None of this, however, need be true. If your second

marriage is running into trouble, you might try to understand the insights and approaches the marriage therapist or counselor uses so that you can judge whether or not you will benefit from such guidance.

Psychiatrist Jerome Frank has probably done more than any other behavioral scientist in attempting to identify what makes therapy work. Here we are using the word "therapy" in a broad sense, since, as we all know, there seems to be an infinite variety of therapeutic methods, from psychoanalysis to drug therapy to group therapy to marital interactional therapy, and so on. People usually seek help only when they are demoralized, he points out, when they have lost confidence in their ability to handle their problems and determine the course of their lives. In some way they feel personally responsible for their distress, no longer able to fall back on the convenient excuse of blaming everyone else except themselves for whatever has gone wrong. He concludes that all therapies exert a beneficial influence by restoring morale, helping us regain hope and command of ourselves and our situations, and that all possess three basic attributes:

1. A trusting, confiding, meaningful relationship with an authority who offers knowledge and experience of value to you.

2. The opportunity to express your thoughts and feelings freely, spontaneously, without fear of being censored or undue concern for consequences.

3. A scheme or formula, a way of interpreting events, that both you and the person whose counsel you have sought share and that serves as the basis for a reconsideration of what you are experiencing so that you can discover new and better ways to handle your situation.

The goal of all therapy is change. You change. The

character of your marriage changes. You bring yourself to a position of being able to make freer choices—the most critical choice, of course, being whether or not to continue the marriage. If you do decide to go on with it, you must learn to make the adjustments necessary to make it work.

The therapist from the start is attempting to clearly define your problems—what they seem to be and what they really are. To do this he must find the answers to some crucial questions.

Just how concerned or upset are you about the marital situation? If you are upset, how is that stress affecting you emotionally? Are you depressed? How does it affect you phsically? Have you lost weight? Does it affect your day-to-day functioning? Are you able to go about your ordinary routine.

What is the present problem? Sex? Bickering and arguing? Lack of affection? A persistent resentment toward each other? Lack of mutual interests and time shared together? Infidelity?

What do you think is at the root of the problem? A wrong marital choice? Do you think that either you or your new partner has changed significantly since the marriage? Are there outside pressures which operate in a destructive way on your relationship?

What is your background, family pattern, education, life experience? What was your former marriage like and why did it break up? What kind of life have you led between marriages?

What is the rest of your life like? How do you get on with your children? What kind of work do you do and are you content with it? What about economic pressures?

In gathering all this information, the therapist often asks for examples in order to get an objective idea of what is really going on. If a woman says her new husband is insensitive, she will be asked to give some instances of this insensitivity. If a man expresses distrust about his new wife's fidelity, he will be asked to explain what evidence, if any, he has for these suspicions.

The therapist's usual procedure is to see each person separately, once or several times, to get as clear a picture as he can of both the marriage itself and the personalities and backgrounds of each person in it. What he is doing is looking for clues, trying to determine which problems come from friction between the couple and which are really the inner conflicts of one or both of the partners that are affecting the relationship. This clarification is critical, since it will determine the recommendations that the therapist will make. For example, if the problem seems primarily in the interaction between the couple, he will probably suggest a number of joint sessions so that both can try to straighten out misunderstandings and communication problems. If one or both are bringing significant individual conflicts to the marriage, he may recommend separate therapy with each before directly dealing with the marriage itself.

Two more vital questions are in the therapist's mind. First, has there been a period of harmony and good interaction between the couple for a significant period of time before the trouble started? The better the relationship had been, before or in the early period of the marriage, the better the chances will be of putting it back on course. Second, he will want to know how committed each of the parties is to the marriage. If both are reasonably committed to making it work and to each other, the outlook should be good. If one or the other is not committed, looking at the consultation as one way of getting out of the marriage or viewing therapy as a means of controlling the other person, the outlook will vary from poor to grim.

Anne Brighton had met her husband two years before their marriage. Her former husband had died suddenly of a heart attack. She was lonely and confused at the time. "I didn't want to marry out of unhappiness," she told her psychiatrist. "So I put David off for a long time, until I felt sure. I still had doubts when I said yes. Panic, even, at times. But I put these feelings aside and agreed to go ahead. Sex was good. We liked the same people. I got on well with David's two children. I respected him."

Anne was startled, therefore, when, within a month after she married David, she began to feel tired, bored, irritable. "I felt trapped, as though I made a terribly wrong decision and couldn't get out of it." She also noticed a change in the way she viewed David. "I started to distrust him. I felt he wasn't telling me the truth, especially about money and about contacts he was having with his former wife. Small habits he had—like using a toothpick after meals or wearing the same pair of underwear two days in a row—things I had paid no attention to before—began to enrage me. I started to look at him as a stranger and someone who turned me off completely. I saw him as a social climber. We fought a lot about this. Sex dropped out entirely."

Anne was convinced that her problem had to be dealt with decisively. She had always been an independent woman. She had already confronted David with her wish to separate, to which he had reacted with a mixture of pleading and anger. "You've got to be out of your mind," he shouted. He suggested she go to a "shrink." She said she had no interest in "I'm O.K., you're not" games, that their marriage was a mistake, that she wanted out. When David broke down and cried and begged her to stay, she felt terribly sorry for him. Her sense of responsibility prevailed and she agreed to see a marriage counselor if he would go too.

"I can't imagine what you can tell me or suggest I do that can change the way things are," Anne concluded helplessly in her first consultation. The psychiatrist said that if he thought there was no future for the two of them together, he would say so but that it was essential for her to keep an open mind. Listening to how convinced Anne was that it could not work, he had serious doubts himself about the prospects for her marriage and had to remind himself that he too should keep an open mind.

When he asked Anne whether there was some specific reason why she had lost respect for David and felt so resentful toward him, she described how David had failed to tell her about a bank loan for fifteen thousand dollars he had taken out a few weeks before they were married. "He was afraid if I thought he didn't have enough money, I wouldn't marry him. It was for school tuitions and to buy furniture for our apartment. Sure, I would have felt less secure if I had known. But it was the deception that I can't stand." Anne had discovered the loan accidentally, discovering one of the repayment slips from the bank on the hall table.

The doctor interviewed David, who could be quite evasive at times. For example, it took three or four questions just to find out something as simple as what kind of work he was doing. This confirmed what Anne had complained about. "David will say he's not sure what he's doing on a particular Saturday afternoon," she described, "and then it will turn out that he had, in fact, already told his children he would probably see them." Part of David's problem was an inability to say no to anyone whose disapproval he feared. It was unintentional, automatic, but it came across as if he were deliberately lying.

It became obvious that David was seriously aggravating the situation because of his own insecurity. He repeatedly would ask Anne if she really loved him, in spite of knowing about her obvious uncertainty about their marriage. This irritated her, and she often found herself unable to answer affirmatively. "I don't know," she would say. Upset by this response, David would then launch into a long monologue, telling Anne how much he loved her, pointing out how impossible and hurtful she was being, asking whether there was someone else. Anne, feeling even more trapped, had an even stronger urge to quit the therapy and just call the whole thing off.

The psychiatrist handled this issue with David very directly. "You're simply going to have to cut it out," he said, "if you hope for any chance for this marriage. Otherwise, you'll drive her away permanently. For someone who had plenty of girlfriends and was married before," the doctor went on, "you have an incredibly strong dependency on Anne. I suspect it's not so much a measure of how much you love her or need her as it is a reaction to being rejected by her. I don't think you can stand the idea that she is disenchanted with you right now, and that's making you push harder and harder to get her back in line. Give her breathing room. Let her have time and privacy to let her real feelings come out." David was, in fact, astonished to hear his behavior described and interpreted in this way. He saw quickly how he was making things worse and began a serious and eventually successful effort to stop pressing Anne.

As he let up, she felt more and more comfortable. By now she had been seeing the psychiatrist twice weekly for two months. She started to look more closely at herself, into her own background and personal attitudes. Because she had been extremely conscientious all her life, her motivations often sprang from guilt. Between marriages and early on in her relationship with David, Anne had had a brief sexual encounter with a man she had then worked with. She had become pregnant. Secretly, she had obtained an abortion. She wanted a child, but not under those circumstances. Abortion was contrary to her personal ethic, but she felt she had no choice but to terminate the pregnancy. Afterward, she began to fear that she might never again be able to have a child, and this fear persisted in spite of her obstetrician's reassurances. She had never told anyone, until now, about this incident.

"I feel a terrible sense of guilt about this still and it makes me want to push David away from me. There's something else I feel guilty about too. I had a lovely relationship with my former husband. We were married only two years before he died. It was awful. We had spent so much time making plans, hoping to have a family. I feel somehow disloyal, marrying again. But I also feel guilty toward David, because no matter how much I cared—I mean care—about him, I don't know if I love him the way I loved before. I feel like a hypocrite."

These revelations—the chance to confide in someone about her abortion, the opportunity to see how unrealistic it was for her to compare her marriage with David with her former marriage, her tremendous need to be "honest" with herself to such a degree that she was perpetually experiencing herself as a "charlatan"—were followed by a significant lifting in her spirits. "I'm beginning to feel some of the affection I used to feel toward Dave. I think things might just work out." Shortly thereafter the two of them went to Bermuda on vacation, thoroughly enjoying each other's company and resuming their sexual relationship.

But an even more profound change in their relationship occurred after Anne, at her therapist's direction, began to consider how her parents' marriage influenced her own expectations of marriage and in particular how she was carrying over problems that she had had with her mother into her own marriage. Anne's mother had always been a very insecure woman, rarely expressing her own thoughts and feelings, frequently the target for the sudden and explosive temper of Anne's father. She was someone Anne could not depend on and trust and certainly not someone she wanted to resemble.

"I came away from childhood convinced that I could only count on myself. In my first marriage, I felt I had found someone I could trust completely. Of course, we hadn't lived together long enough for that to be really tested. I see that now. After his death, I was convinced more than ever I should never put all my eggs in one basket, and this made me feel vulnerable, outraged by David's indirectedness."

Anne continued to see the psychiatrist twice a week for four months. She then cut back to one visit weekly for another three months. By this time things had improved so much that she could feel free to go it on her own, always knowing that she could come back for a visit should she want to. During her therapy David came to see the doctor once a month, primarily working on his need to be more forthright in his communication, to increase his understanding of himself, of Anne, and to obtain some practical suggestions about how he might handle his former wife and children in a better way.

During one of the few joint sessions that Anne and David had together with the therapist, Anne said, "You're still the same person you have always been, David, and I love you. But I can see you're trying and that's what matters. I really think we're going to make it."

Sometimes a therapist has a pretty good idea, from the very beginning, of what the outcome will be. He knows that things will work out. Sometimes, as in Anne's situation, the outcome is considerably less certain, and it is one of the professional's greatest satisfactions when his original doubts prove to be reversed. He always has to be careful himself not to prejudge or be influenced by his own biases. Anne's psychiatrist, for example, while he neither liked or disliked David, did find him occasionally irritating. David would assume the tone of a colleague, calling on the telephone from time to time, to report on Anne's behavior and emotional state. There was a touch of arrogance in this approach, and the therapist had to be careful not to let his impatience with David influence his work with Anne. When he felt the time was right—and therapy is very much a matter of timing—he made it clear to David that just because Anne was coming regularly and more often, she should not be considered any more or less sick than David. "In fact," the doctor commented, "I don't think of either of you as sick. Nor is it a matter of who is right or wrong in your type of situation. The plan I have set up is the one I think will work best."

In Anne and David's problem, the most serious difficulty seemed to arise from Anne's own inner turmoil and her projection of this onto her marriage. David's reactions did not help, nor was he by any means problem-free. But his own conflicts were more peripheral to the marital problem for which the psychiatrist had been consulted.

There are times when the problem is clearly due to difficulties in the interaction between the couple. A thirty-four-year-old remarried woman and her husband who had never been married before consulted a therapist because, after two years of marriage and in spite of a high degree of compatibility of interests, respect for each other, similar backgrounds, and an initially good sexual adjustment, their sexual life had completely disappeared. They found themselves bickering repeatedly and becoming increasingly critical of each other. She felt her husband was undemonstrative, too concerned with himself and his career, uninterested in sex, and unwilling to talk things out. "Maybe my needs are just greater than his. But there's no excuse for his refusal to talk with me about our problems."

Her husband's position was quite different. "Whenever I wanted to make love, she would put me off for an hour or two. There was always something she wanted to do first. By the time she was ready, I had lost interest. Naturally I felt rejected."

"It's you who have been rejecting me," his wife interjected.

"Not true," he insisted. "I think actions are more important than words, while you think we should talk and talk and talk."

During a half-dozen joint sessions with the therapist, this couple was able to significantly restructure their relationship. The most critical step involved helping each see that the other was not really rejecting the other at all. Rather they were too sensitive to any actions or words that could be misinterpreted as a sign of rejection. The husband was encouraged to express his feelings more directly, especially when angry, and to let his wife know how he felt rather than smoldering for weeks, drawing further and further away from any close contact with her. The wife, in turn, was advised to cut back on her need to confront him again and again with those things about himself that she was most unhappy about and wanted him to change. "Your husband knows what they are," the therapist pointed out. "The more you chide him about them, the more stubbornly they become entrenched. A lot of people are that way. Let up a little. We'll discuss them here. See if you can't offer a bit more encouragement and less criticism."

Some therapists use videotape playback techniques with

couples, so that their discussions are recorded throughout and at any point they can stop the machine and show a couple, directly, immediately, how they act and behave with a forcefulness that words often do not have.

The problems that couples present are not necessarily complex and deeply rooted. Not infrequently, what seems insumountable turns out to have quite a simple answer, one that the couple themselves simply failed to spot. As one forty-eight-year-old remarried woman described, "My husband and I had both been married before. We knew how painful divorce could be. We thought we had made right choices. But within a few months after our marriage, we started to have awful fights—over nothing. At a dinner party, for example, I'd make some remark that seemed innocent enough. My husband would take offense and contradict me. I'd be hurt. He'd say nothing more about it until we got home. Then all hell would break loose, with him screaming profanities at me and me going to the bedroom and slamming the door closed and crying—but never in front of him. Then I'd lose control too and go back downstairs and we'd yell and scream at each other until we were both too tired to go on.

"We'd make up the next day, but a few weeks later there'd be another scene. We couldn't get to the bottom of it. We read all kinds of books. Was it sex? The pressure of so many grown children and their problems? Financial strains? Or was it more basic, some kind of imcompatibility, and the idea of that really scared us both.

"It was only after we talked it over with an outsider—our minister in this case—that we recognized that the cause of the problem was drinking. Neither of us are alcoholics. That's not the point. But two or three drinks could unpredictably make both of us very touchy. My husband especially would misinterpret what I said as if

I were attacking him. After a few drinks I found it impossible to control my feelings, particularly a self-righteous kind of rage. We just didn't think of it. After these discussions we watched our habits over the next six months and had only one real fight."

Of course, there are times when it is apparent that a second marriage should not continue. When there are no children involved and no long history of closeness and a shared life together, it is less complicated for a couple to admit that they should not remain married. The therapist's task may be to help them to accept that they acted in haste or out of poor judgment. The middle-aged man, for example, who, in a desperate effort to regain his youth, marries an immature girl in her early twenties, only to find her carrying on sexual relationships with some of her old boyfriends within a few months after their marriage; the thirty-seven-year-old divorcee who, in search of emotional security, marries a forty-five-year-old man, attractive, charming, personable, she has known only a short time, only to discover that he has lied to her about his past—his wife did not leave him because of another man but because he had a serious drinking problem at the time, and instead of having a secure job with good retirement benefits he is forty-thousand dollars in debt and on the verge of being fired—these are typical of the kind of situations that marital therapists encounter where they conclude that it would be best for all concerned just to call things off as quickly and as painlessly as possible.

But sometimes it is difficult to diagnose by yourself whether or not your problems are irreversible. If your second marriage has run into trouble and your own efforts to solve things are not paying off, consider some kind of counseling. If you do not know whether you need it or not or whether you would benefit from it, find out by asking a professional. Don't let the cost hold you back. There are numerous services available at a nominal fee, and remember successful counseling is often a good deal less expensive than a divorce.

If you do decide to seek professional help, choose wisely and with care. There can be risks. The experience and competence of the professional whose advice you seek is critical. As one forty-four-year-old man, twice divorced, reported: "I had therapy for several years, in my early thirties, before my first divorce. I feel it helped me a lot. But when my second marriage ran into trouble, I went back to my analyst for help. He said he would take me on again, if I wanted. But I'd have to come several times a week for at least a year. And he refused to see my wife.

"She, in turn, had gone to a neurologist who claimed to be a marriage expert. He asked to see me. I went. For an hour I sat there and listened to him lecture and harangue me for being negligent, for not treating her right, for not spending enough time with her, for not letting her have enough of a say in things. He told me there was nothing wrong with my wife, that I was the problem. He refused to make another appointment—not that I wanted one—and told me to go home and do what he had told me to do. I later found out that he gave the exact same advice to the husband of every woman who consulted him. He envisioned himself as some kind of woman-saver. The hospital staff he belonged to insisted on his retirement shortly afterward because of impaired judgment due to aging. But the damage was done. In my wife's mind she was convinced that I had mistreated her and it was all my fault. In a couple of months my second marriage went down the drain."

There are certain precautions you can take to increase your chances of finding a suitable and effective consultant or therapist. In the first place, get a good recommendation from someone you can trust, a clergyman, your family physician, a friend in the profession, people you know who have been helped by marital therapy. Check credentials. It is true that a person's professional training and experience alone don't tell you the whole story. There are some therapists with high-ranking positions in hospitals and university centers who may be inept, and there are some who do not have a long list of publications or honors to their credit who are uniquely skilled at handling people. Nonetheless, it is naïve to ignore reputation.

For the initial consultation, at least, be sure the person you select is truly eclectic in his or her approach to your problems. He should not be a rabid devotee of some exclusive school of therapy. He should be able to evaluate not only your marriage but also you and your partner individually as well, in order to sort out the pieces and offer you the best options for the solution of your dilemma.

Finally, there is no test like your own evaluation of the person and his approach. If you intuitively feel confidence that this is the right person and that you can form a good relationship with him, you are probably on the right track. Expect him to listen attentively and intelligently and not jump to hasty conclusions; at the same time, expect him to make some contributions by way of advice or explanation and not to hide behind a façade of silence most of the time. Nor should he insist, directly or covertly, that you have to contract to be sick in order to obtain the help you need. A good therapist will be just as interested in what is right as what is wrong. He will also be skilled at keeping a confidence. Whether the same therapist works with both you and your spouse, seeing you individually or together, or whether, because of his personal preference or the special nature of your problem, the therapist feels that each of you should be seen by different therapists, he should not and will not betray your intimate revelations. It is not ethical. It is also not good practice. If, after a few visits, you and your spouse feel that you have chosen incorrectly, don't just give up and quit therapy itself. Quit this situation and find another one more suitable.

What if you want to get some help and your partner is opposed or at best indifferent? This is not the best of situations, but it is a mistake to assume that your partner's reluctance indicates, in and of itself, that he or she doesn't care enough to bother. Your spouse may be afraid. He or she may not be oriented toward psychological solutions or may have been burned in the past. Then again your partner may not think that the problem, whatever it is, is as serious as you do, perhaps justifiably, perhaps not. There is still no reason why you cannot obtain some valuable insights and direction for handling your problem from a competent professional on your own. You may then be able to find ways to stimulate your partner into following your lead. Many people are, naturally, quite threatened by the thought that the person they love wants some outside advice, experiencing it more as a personal rejection than as a move toward improvement. And so it is important, if you are the one who prefers not to seek professional direction, not to assume that your partner's wish or intention to do so means that he or she does not love you or wishes to discontinue the marriage.

Remember, there are other options to choose among. If you do not regard your particular problems as too serious, you may find the answers you require in some of the marriage encounter and discussion groups in which millions of people have participated over the past decade or more. The search for improvement itself is a major spur toward making things better. Just be sure, if you do this kind of soul-searching, that you avoid those groups that require you to bare everything in public as part of the process. Discretion is still a valuable virtue, and feelings or experiences revealed in a moment of enthusiasm or great emotion may be hard to forget or forgive later on.

The ultimate goal of all therapy is, of course, to enable each of us to develop ways of solving our problems on our own as much as we can, while still recognizing when we have to turn to others for help. Recalling Jerome Frank's hypothesis of what all therapies have in common—someone to confide in, trust, an atmosphere of hope wherein you can express your feelings and ideas freely and be heard, a common language and shared values—there is no reason why each of us cannot strive to cultivate these in the relationship with the person to whom we are married, so that much of the time we can between ourselves resolve the issues that arise as they arise. The experience of therapists tells us that, in the end, there is no substitute for an honest and determined commitment to each other and to the marriage and the freedom to give of ourselves to each other in a generous and loving way. This is a lesson that those in second marriages should learn by heart.

17

All Successful Marriages are Second Marriages

The need for renewal—a periodic recommitment by both husband and wife to each other and to their relationship—is a critical part of every marriage. Anne Morrow Lindbergh described this process in terms of the shifts and changes that all couples face: "When you love someone you do not love them all the time, in exactly that same way, from moment to moment. It is an impossibility. It is even a lie to pretend to. And yet this is exactly what most of us demand. . . . How can one learn to live through the ebb-tides of one's existence?"

How indeed, when we live in a society whose values are hazy and in which difficult life situations are dealt with by simply avoiding them rather than learning to confront them and search out solutions. And so it is not surprising to find divorce and a fresh start often having real appeal, especially when many of us share the bias expressed by Albert Finney in the film *Two for the Road*. In a number of scenes, Finney turns to Audrey Hepburn, points to some middle-aged couple sitting at a nearby table in a restaurant who are eating in silence, and repeats disparagingly, "That's marriage."

Many marriages, first as well as second, end unnecessarily because couples cannot cope successfully with the demand for renewal. Certainly there are plenty of instances when a marriage should end: when, for example, the original choices prove to be faulty and dangerous, when one or both of the partners is psychologically unable or unwilling to meet the responsibilities of the marital commitment, or when some serious and destructive problem, such as uncontrollable alcoholism or repeated brutality, defies resolution. But, with greater social freedom, more and more marriages are falling apart simply because the people involved are not even aware of the fact that it takes courage, will, resilience, and imagination to make any marriage endure and flourish. If you think that by leaving one unhappy marriage and marrying again you can escape the ebb and flow that Anne Lindbergh describes, you are not only mistaken but run the high risk of failing again. For second marriages are just as subject to the pressures that stem from change as first ones are.

Whether this is your first or second marriage, if you marry in your mid-twenties or early thirties and you expect to stay married to this person for the rest of your life, you are talking about a probable life-span of forty years or more for your relationship. That is an incredibly long time. It is the distance between the First World War and the space probe to Mars. It is the time between standing before a church altar in the 1920s as bride and groom, vowing to be true to each other forever, and, now in the 1970s, living in a one-bedroom condominium on Florida's west coast, hearing about once close friends passing on and hoping that your son and daughter will bring their families to see you before much more time passes.

To get there you will have to survive many changes. Let's ignore for the moment the enormous social and environmental changes that will take place and consider only those that will occur within you yourself and in your relationship with your partner. Over the years you are bound to cultivate new points of view, letting go of obsolete attitudes and behavior patterns, modifying some of your values. You may gain in wisdom. You may become more responsible. Having been very practical and pragmatic, you may slowly come to value sentiment and begin to pay more attention to the quality of your relationships with others. Perhaps you have always given in to your moods and emotions. You might start to exert a certain amount of control over these and become more logical in the way you handle situations, thinking before you act. Once you thought that being a wife and mother was enough; now it does not seem to be, and you feel you should find an occupation that will fulfill your potential talents. Once you were convinced that becoming head of a department at a university was an essential goal; now you think the price is too high, as your freedom and self-realization become of greater importance to you.

This pattern of individual personal evolution is never a straight line forward. Unlike school days, when we moved from one grade to another sequentially, psychological growth involves episodes of failure, backsliding—falling apart, if you will—in order to reshape ourselves and again move on to new levels. This process is stressful, to say the least, and during such periods of change we may have to do everything we can to keep our wits about us and to prevent the strain from unduly injuring or wrecking our marriages.

Add the relationship between you and your partner to this picture and you can see, at once, that the quality of your marriage will be seriously affected. You may support each other in this process or, conversely, make it more difficult. Another crucial factor further complicates this situation: Your marital relationship itself, with its own identity, has its own pattern of evolution. Just as we can identify crises that individuals go through at various phases in life, so too can we recognize major points of transition that marriages go through, times when stress is at a peak and the need for renewal is urgent. If this is your first marriage and you are young, you will inevitably go through all these phases together if the marriage lasts. If this is your second marriage, you will still be faced with the same predictable periods of readjustment, disruption, and renewal, although just how and when these will occur depends on what time in each of your lives you reenter marriage.

There are basically three major stages in the lifetime of a marriage. The first stage starts the moment you marry and continues until you have children. The committing of yourself to another person and a way of life immediately sets off a series of psychological vibrations. For a while it may be thrilling to be a couple, Mr. and Mrs., with "our car," "our home," "our friends." But it is also a bit frightening. Even if you have been living together before, the fact that you are now officially married alters the nature of your involvement. Inevitably, the events of the first year of a new marriage bring on some degree of anxiety and depression, simply because, in order to move into this new kind of life, you've had to give up many things you valued in the one you were leading. The loneliness is gone, but so is the independence. You are no longer as free as you were, now having to account to someone else for your presence, time, attention, and love.

People entering first marriages are often unprepared for this stress because of romantic and sexual blinders that keep them from seeing anything else. Therefore, as their initial excitement subsides, they can become quite confused by the strains that creep in. In second marriages, people are often misled into thinking that, because they have been married before, they can necessarily look ahead to a much smoother adjustment. And when trouble appears in the form of impatience, conflicts of interest, hurt feelings, whatever, they may mistakenly assume that they made the wrong choice of partner rather than being able to attribute the troubles or discord to a normal response to the stresses they are encountering. Only by knowing how to shake off negative feelings and to renew the commitment to each other during this initial period of either a first or second marriage can you make it really work.

The next stage in the usual course of a marriage begins when children come. If the couple has successfully weathered their first year or two together—and increasingly they are finding this hard to do—then they are usually ready to start building a family. A child is born, though not without a previous period that blends the joy of anticipation with anxiety about financial consequences and worries about the child's health. No more ski weekends or sharing houses with childless couples at the beach. No more slipping out for a pizza and a glass of wine at ten o'clock at night or deciding at the last minute to see a movie. The odor of diapers creeps through the tiny apartment, and by the time this disappears there is the constant and never ceasing fear that the small child, crawling around, trying to stand on its own two feet, climbing, will inadvertently head for an open window or a box of Ajax under the kitchen sink. Small wonder that the incidence of nervous breakdowns among women with young children at home is extremely high.

But other psychological shifts occur as well. On many

levels, becoming a parent forces inner change. Unconsciously, for example, each of us has an image of what it is to be a mother or a father. This is based on our identification with our own parents. Regardless of whether it is a model we prefer or one that we reject, it is there, and the arrival of children activates it as surely as flipping the wall switch turns on the light. Certain traits of your mother or father slip into your own mannerisms and attitudes, not only in how you relate to your children but how you deal with your partner as well. It is as if, invisibly, four other people now occupy the household and the struggle to be yourself will include the need to dispel these shadows, a task you can undertake only when you can appreciate their compelling presence.

The shadows and the realities mix to produce tension and depression for a while. Your zest for life may not be what it was. You are bored, irritable. You worry more about money. Your sexual ardor is less. You are tired, feeling harassed. It is easy to blame it all on your marriage.

Becoming parents is a stressful event that some people in second marriages never have to face. But not always. Marriages in which one partner has been married before but the other has not are quite common. A man in his thirties or forties with children by a previous marriage might, for example, marry a woman who has never been married and who wants her own children. Although he has already been through some of the stresses triggered by parenthood, she has not. He may readily misinterpret her normal reactions to motherhood as evidence that she has lost interest in him, while she, in turn, may incorrectly think that, because her husband's reaction to the child's arrival is less intense than her own, he does not care enough about his new family.

A further shift—though still part of the child-oriented family—takes place when the last small child marches off to school and continues as the youngsters grow up and enter their teenage years. Even though you may welcome your new liberty, you cannot avoid experiencing a sense of loss.

In a much acclaimed novel *The War Between the Tates*, the author presents a graphic picture of a woman who realizes that she is somewhat repelled by her adolescent children. Certainly it is no secret that having teenage children in the home can cause considerable turmoil. Yet the drama of it has been, in general, exaggerated, for there are many families in which adolescent boys and girls are interesting in their growing perception of the world, helpful around the house, and a real pleasure to be with. But the pull toward adulthood, rooted in the teenager's very nature, makes it a difficult and anxiety-provoking age. You lie awake at night wondering if they will get home all right. You may not be sure how to discuss sex with them or what to expect of their behavior. There are bound to be arguments and scenes, as your youngsters tell you they know more about life than you do and you find yourself arguing with your husband or wife, each claiming that the other is somehow responsible for the children's appalling behavior.

Then, suddenly, it is over, and the next major stage in marriage begins. By now you are probably in your mid-forties. The family is gone. You and your partner are left to deal with each other, face to face, alone for the first time in years. These are the middle years, referred to as such largely because of the extended life-span that modern medicine has given us. For now, what once would have been considered the onset of age is instead looked on as the door to a new life free from old responsiblities, tuitions, and the nagging ambitions that made you feel you had to keep pushing ahead indefinitely. If, at this point, you are not too bruised by all you have been through, and if you and your partner are still together, the time has come for you to start designing the sort of life you want for yourselves in the unpredictable years to come.

Where do you want to live? How? Are either or both of you so caught up in careers that you have little time for each other? What do you really have in common? And when, in a few years, you retire, what will you do to keep active? What will your economic situation be like? Then there's health to be considered. Pretty soon the specters of heart disease and cancer and arthritis and a host of other problems will close in on you. And, as if that weren't enough, while you are struggling to cope with these issues, one or more of your parents is likely to fall ill and die. Again depression moves in, and when it is not recognized and handled correctly, all the interpersonal conflicts and misunderstandings that go along with depression can undermine your marriage. It is no coincidence that the divorce rate soars within a couple of years following the death of a significant family member, since it is a direct outcome of the emotional changes that people go through after such a loss.

Now, if you feel you haven't lived enough, you may be strongly tempted to throw everything to the winds and try to use what time you have left to do all those things you always wanted to do if you only had had the chance. Whether you end up doing these things together or apart depends entirely on whether you can, once more, renew your commitment to each other.

A successful marriage, therefore, is essentially a series of remarriages that take place as husbands and wives move from one stage of their relationship to the next. And while anticipating these periods of stress and change is crucial, just knowing is unfortunately not enough. What we all need is a philosophy, a basic point of view, to survive these disruptions in intimacy. For example, we should understand that the growth of the relationship between a husband and wife takes time and must be actively nurtured. Ignored, like a plant that goes unwatered, it will inevitably die. Caring, giving, sharing—these are some of the terms we commonly employ to describe this nurturing process. Summed up, it can be placed under the heading of love and commitment.

But caring, by itself, is not enough. We also must have the resilience necessary to absorb the impact of the shocks that transitional periods produce. There are times when our relationship will fall apart, for the very purpose of being reconstructed in a stronger and more relevant form. Such a cycle of death and rebirth, although part of mankind's inherent history, unfortunately goes against our contemporary philosophy, trained as we have been to worship success and be intolerant of failure. We have also been conditioned to be good consumers, building our things—including our lives—so that they wear out. In other words, we are no longer culturally oriented toward renewal and repair, and so we have trouble viewing marriage as the paradox it is: an enduring commitment and, at the same time, periodic recommitment.

Putting together what might seem at first contradictory elements—risk and uncertainty on the one hand, conviction and dedication on the other—calls for an insightful and creative mind. Fortunately, such insight and creativity are potentials most of us have within us, and they are qualities we can cultivate with practice.

A capacity for insight means that you can learn things about yourself and the reality around you of which you were not previously aware and that you can then implement these discoveries effectively. For instance, if you have been selfish, always putting your own needs first, insight is the process that will enable you to recognize this fault and, with some effort, abandon it. If your marriage is being torn apart by a number of pressures, as is especially true at points of transition, you can find out where these pressures are originating, what their true nature is, and how to deal with them appropriately. It has been said that the basis of good medical treatment is making the right diagnosis. Like a physician, once you know what is wrong, you will be in a stronger position to correct it. Until then you are more likely to thrash about in the dark, tilting at windmills and doing quite a bit of damage in the process. Once you know what is right, where your opportunities are, you will be able to take advantage of them. Insight, like radar, will enable you to sort fact from fiction and help you choose valid directions to move in.

Insight's twin is creativity. Contrary to common opinion, the ability to be creative is not restricted to the development of some special talent. It is a personality characteristic that applies to all aspects of living. Creativity has been correctly defined as nothing more or less than the ability to look at things in new and different ways and effectively consider unexpected options. By being creative we can often find rather surprising answers to our personal problems and marital dilemmas which, at the moment of first consideration, seem unsolvable.

In other words, creativity is the process of exchanging one perception or vision of a situation for another. Its relevance to the reconstruction of marriage after a period of change is instantly apparent. Ordinarily we tend to hold onto obsolete images of ourselves and other people and situations, images that no longer apply. When you rearrange the furniture in your home, you will, for a while afterward, find yourself reaching for objects that are no longer where they were and bumping into tables or chairs in the dark. After years of living together many couples react to each other as they once were, not as they are now. Updating is a creative act, for it involves forfeiting old and no longer relevant ways of seeing something in favor of more contemporary and accurate ones. When the time to recommit yourself to your marriage and your partner arrives, as it will every so many years, you have to shake loose of residues that interfere with your seeing things as they are in the present in order to make such a recommitment meaningful. It is not that you will forget either the good or the bad of prior years. But you will find that, at this moment of renewal, the past will be no more real than a dream you may have experienced once a long time ago. And only then will you be free to work together to create a new kind of future.

The best way to insure that you have the creativity necessary to cope with these critical turning points in your marriage is to introduce a creative spirit to your relationship from the very beginning and keep it alive throughout the years. You can do this by emphasizing the attitudes and behavior patterns conducive to such a spirit and minimizing those that interfere. For example, it is essential for both of you to stay in touch with your own feelings as well as those of your partner and to be as honest and direct in your communications as possible. It is important not to allow resentments to smolder beneath the surface. Instead, try to develop a facility for dealing with conflict in a forthright way and learn the art of forgiveness. Forgiveness is, in fact, a highly creative experience, involving a letting go of hurt feelings and a reuniting after a break in intimacy, without—as many incorrectly assume—the need to push out of memory what has transpired.

Many couples tend to dwell on the same trouble spots,

thinking about them over and over again, worrying about them, rehashing them in conversations. This habit is the direct antithesis of the creative approach to solutions, since it almost always leads you to reinforce the impasses you ran into before. You must learn how to let go of issues long enough for them to simmer, in the unconscious, while you are searching for new answers.

As a couple, you should not be too dependent on the opinions of others, struggling to win their acceptance, darting this way and that to avoid rejection. The more you can develop a style of living that is truly your own, the less your marriage will become contaminated by values and expectations that are not only unsuited to you but nowadays often detrimental to your relationship.

Give each other a chance to think out loud. Don't jump to pass judgment on the value of each other's ideas. Nothing blocks creative thinking more surely than premature criticism, whether you are aiming it at your partner's ideas or your own.

Virtue is an old-fashioned word, but its meaning is timeless. Aspects of virtue—courage, integrity, and loyalty, for instance—are essential for a healthy and resilient marital bond, even as manipulation, control, dishonesty, and cowardice readily destroy it. And, of course, there is nothing like a good sense of humor to stimulate your relationship and serve at moments of tension as a vital catalyst to restore the neccessary perspective.

You will find it invaluable to actually practice at being creative whenever you're faced with situations that demand unforeseen solutions. With practice you can develop a flexible approach to your life so that when really important crises come you will be ready to face them effectively. For example, we know that when we're trying to solve a problem one good approach consists of stating the problem in a different way. Redefine it. Rephrase your questions. If you have been married for a couple of years and you think you want out of the marriage, instead of just asking yourself, "Should I get a divorce?" ask instead, "Why am I unable to release myself from old hurts and resentments? What were my original expectations of marriage? How have they changed? Does it make sense for me to be on my own? What could I do, specifically, to make things better?" You may be surprised by the answers.

Once you state your problem in a different way, then you can employ one of the basic rules for creative thinking by coming up with a long list of ideas. The more you come up with, the greater your chances of discovering some that are truly better. For example, you and your husband or wife may be trying to come to terms with disagreements you have about how your children are being reared. One of you wants a more disciplined home environment, the other a more loosely structured one. Every time you try to settle this, you get nowhere. So you start to brainstorm the subject together, creating a list of forty or more ideas related to the problem, practical ones, wild and silly ones. You may eventually discover that the dispute has more to do with the way each of you were brought up than with the needs of your particular child or your current thoughts on the subject. Then you may for the first time be able to shape a common attitude that will permit the two of you to be consistent with each other in dealing with the children in your home.

From time to time you might distance yourself from your problems, geographically, mentally. This encourages fresh points of view. By the same token you could put yourselves in situations that are likely to stimulate new ideas and surround yourself with people who offer constructive input into your relationship, while keeping your contact with those who enjoy sabotaging it to a minimum.

You needn't allow what you do together to interfere with your own individuality. Everyone needs privacy, time alone, a chance to be yourself. But neither should you permit your own personal interests to keep you from sharing. Every couple needs to be together.

Times change. People change. The more creative you are, the more you can adapt to these changes, and the easier it will be for you to understand the seeming contradiction that marriage is a permanent relationship interlaced by a series of endings and new beginnings. Moreover, when the need arises, you will be better able to renew it.

Take out your old wedding pictures now and look at them. You may not have done this for years. How young everyone looks. It was raining that morning, but by the time you reached the church, the sun had come out. Whatever happened to Ruth? She was one of your bridesmaids. You haven't heard from her in ten years. Whatever happened to Paul? He was your best man. Who would have thought he would have turned out the way he did? Where did you go afterward on your wedding trip? You may have to think for a moment to remember.

A picture of your children falls out. Polaroid. Taken when you were all together at Christmas at your parents' house. How small they look. You keep playing with the idea that it would be fun to go back in time, for just a little while, like the girl in Thornton Wilder's *Our Town*. Next weekend you'll be going to the christening of your first grandchild.

Very busy now, at the peak of your career. Very busy now, taking care of the house and working part time at the travel agency. Sometimes, when you go out to dinner together, there really isn't too much to say because it's all been said for the moment, so you look at the menu and order wine and sit together in pleasant and comfortable silence.

And you have been married at least four times, each time to the same person, without the legal formalities of separation and going through any ceremonies. The last time it happened was just after your father died. You were very upset. At forty-five you began to feel that life had passed you by in so many ways and to wonder, seriously, whether your husband, who was working such long hours, might have had a girlfriend on the side. He didn't. But he had just been passed over for an important promotion that same year and often seemed so hurt, resentful, feeling unappreciated by the company to which he had devoted so many years. The two of you talked seriously about the possibility of divorce. Neither of you were happy. The children were grown and gone.

But you got things worked out. The grief of your father's death passed. You were distracted from your own problems by a brief but serious illness in one of your children. Your husband decided that there was still time to start out on a business venture of his own. You went to work in the travel agency. The two of you decided to take a trip together, three weeks in a rented Peugot through the French countryside, to get some distance and regain perspective. You had a lot to build on. Sitting in the little café, near the Dordogne, laughing at some private joke, suddenly you both stopped the conversation and reached out for each other's hand, and your fourth marriage began.

Times change. People change. We may wonder sometimes whether the stress and strain isn't too much and whether married life, as we have known it, is headed for oblivion. But we should not be misled by divorce statistics and the popular interpretations of them. The fact that our culture now presents us with a number of options—living alone, living married, divorcing, and remarrying, living together without the formality of marriage—simply means that, in keeping with the contemporary emphasis placed on individual freedom, we now have the privilege of choosing the kind of life that suits us best.

It would be a serious mistake to jump to the conclusion that the widespread unhinging that seems to have taken place in so many of our traditional institutions, including marriage, means their end. Viewed historically, such trends have an extremely short life-span. Living in the center of it, we may be overly impressed by it, but if, following one of the rules for creative insight—distancing—we can climb to a nearby hill and gain enough perspective to see what is taking place, we may begin to view this upheaval in a different light, seeing it as an evolutionary process that, in the end, is going somewhere, even if we are not sure quite where.

To build a better structure, the old one has to come apart for a while. This is what seems to be happening to marriage. If one thing characterizes our century above all others, it is the dramatic expansion of our knowledge and awareness of not only physical forces but psychological and social ones as well. It is as if we are engaged in a race against time, trying desperately to catch up with the strange and complex world we have created for ourselves.

Basically, however, what we seem to be searching for is what mankind has always sought—an increased ability to survive. And in order to succeed we are now dimly aware of the fact that we will have to become wiser, more sensible, more honest, more capable of loving. Creating better marriages can be seen as an essential part of this movement and our surest way to pass on this legacy of wisdom and compassion to our children and the generations to come.

Index